D1539425

★★ A Cartoon History of ★★

United States
Foreign Policy

★★ From 1945 to the Present ★★

★★ A Cartoon History of ★★

United States Foreign Policy

★★ From 1945 to the Present ★★

**By Nancy King and the Editors of
the Foreign Policy Association**

With an Introduction by Richard Reeves

PHAROS BOOKS
A SCRIPPS HOWARD COMPANY
NEW YORK

Copyright © 1991 by the Foreign Policy Association

All rights reserved. No part of this book may be reproduced in any form or by any means without written permission of the publisher.

First published in 1991.

Library of Congress Cataloging-in-Publication Data
King, Nancy, 1957-
    A cartoon history of United States foreign policy from 1945 to the present / by Nancy King and the editors of the Foreign Policy Association.
        p.   cm.
    ISBN 0-88687-535-8 : $24.95. — ISBN 0-88687-534-X (pbk.) : $12.95
    1. United States—Foreign relations—1945- —Caricatures and cartoons. 2. American wit and humor, Pictorial. I. Foreign Policy Association. II. Title.
    E744.K47   1991
    327.73—dc20   90-47090
                                                                                        CIP

Cover design: Nancy Carey
Book design: Suzanne Reisel

Printed in the United States of America

Pharos Books
A Scripps Howard Company
200 Park Avenue
New York, New York 10166

10 9 8 7 6 5 4 3 2 1

Contents

Acknowledgments

Many individuals, organizations, and sources contributed to making this book possible, and it is a pleasure for the Foreign Policy Association to acknowledge their roles:

Toni Mendez, projects chairlady of the Newspaper Features Council, who was the inspiration for the collaboration between the Newspaper Features Council and the Foreign Policy Association on this cartoon history book; we thank her for her wit, enthusiasm, and, above all, her friendship;

the special Newspaper Features Council committee on the cartoon history project—Tony Auth, John Brewer, the late Milton Caniff, Willard Colston, Joseph F. D'Angelo, Robert I. Greenberg, David Hendin, John P. McMeel, Richard S. Newcombe, Robert S. Reed, Mort Walker, and Nanette Wiser—who offered advice and encouragement, and all the other members of the Newspaper Features Council;

Catherine T. Walker, executive director of the Newspaper Features Council, who helped publicize our search for cartoons, obtained reprint permissions from NFC members, and provided invaluable advice throughout the preparation of the manuscript;

Gaiti Ali, assistant editor of the Foreign Policy Association, who quietly, efficiently and doggedly tracked down cartoons, cartoonists, and copyright holders; and, most important of all,

the cartoonists who supplied the indispensable ingredient for this book, their cartoons.

For the cartoons of the 1980s, we are indebted chiefly to the staff of the White House News Summary. While director there, Ben Jarratt created the "Friday Follies," a weekly compilation of editorial cartoons circulated to White House officials. Bruce Wilmot, who succeeded Jarratt as director, made seven years' worth of these files—and a copy machine—available to us. Without their help, this would be a far weaker book. The New York Public Library Collection was also a rich resource.

Special thanks also go to Mitch Berger of *Bull's Eye* magazine for his frequent and helpful advice, and to Larry Wright, who ran a well-timed blurb for us in the

Association of American Editorial Cartoonists' newsletter. Thanks also to Dennis B. Ryan, who has an impressive collection, and to Richard Samuel West, former editor of *Target,* the political cartoon quarterly, who was kind enough to read the manuscript and provided useful comments.

The main historical sources drawn upon were Thomas A. Bailey's *A Diplomatic History of the American People,* Thomas G. Paterson's *American Foreign Policy: A History Since 1900,* and Walter LaFeber, Richard Pollenberg and Nancy Woloch's *The American Century.*

The Foreign Policy Association is a private, nonprofit, nonpartisan educational organization. For over seventy years, the association has worked to stimulate wider interest, greater understanding and more effective participation by American citizens in world affairs. FPA sponsors a wide variety of programs and publications analyzing the problems of American foreign policy. It works closely with many other public and private organizations and with the nation's schools and colleges in its educational effort. The association strives to air different viewpoints impartially; it advocates none.

—The Editors

Introduction

What do you give to the man who really does have everything, including the most powerful and glamorous job in the world?

A political cartoon. Preferably one that makes him look good.

That, at any rate, was what the president of the Soviet Union, Mikhail Gorbachev, decided to give the president of the United States, George Bush, when they met at the summit in Helsinki, Finland, on September 9, 1990, to discuss such things as war in the Middle East and the future of the world. He gave the American a drawing called "Knockout," showing the two of them, Bush and Gorbachev, as boxers with their hands held high in victory, by a referee whose head is the globe, over the knocked-out hulk of a monster called the "Cold War."

There's always a fifty-fifty chance that anyone, president or pauper, will like a cartoon. Of course, there's also a fifty-fifty chance they won't like it. That's the whole idea: you get it or you don't; you like it or you hate it. A few deft lines, a word or two, and a little drawing by the right man or woman can be worth more than a thousand words or a thousand pages of analysis in *The New York Times,* or *Le Monde,* or *Pravda.*

God, how I envy them! (Like much great work, cartooning seems easy if you're not the one who has to do it.) During the time I was writing thousands and thousands of words for *The New York Times* in the 1960s and the '70s, the big stories were the war in Vietnam and Watergate. A few years later I flipped through a little book like this one—a collection of the cartoons of Herbert Block (Herblock) of *The Washington Post*—and I suddenly realized that he, and his readers or viewers or fans, understood what was actually happening long before I and my most celebrated colleagues. That didn't make me happy, quite the opposite, but it did make me understand the power of a discipline that makes the creator choose. You can't really fudge it in a few words. There were two sides to every story I wrote. There was one side in Herb's work: good or bad, right or wrong, black or white. Admiring the work in this book, which I do very much, I was reminded of one of the lines that has stuck with me from another rather direct art, musical comedy. The words I remember were by Tevye, the Jewish tailor in *Fiddler on the Roof,* when he learns his youngest daughter wants to marry a Russian cossack, the fearsome and feared enemy of his people: "On the other hand, there is no other hand."

So the pointed and unequivocal work of the best cartoonists is collected in books, and it should be, and our on-the-one-hand, on-the-other-hand musings are usually eaten by computers. Perhaps that evens the score. Political cartoonists, I believe, are born, not made. Political correspondents and columnists are usually made, a manufacturing process that often includes the best schools and better connections, the best dinner parties and better connections. The money and acclaim, more often than not, come to those of us articulate in defining the other hand.

"Do you want to meet Don Wright?" a friend asked me late one night in 1972 when we had stopped by his office at the *Miami News* to pick up something.

"Sure," I said. "It's not every day, or night, that you meet a Pulitzer Prize-winning cartoonist.

The place was dark and seemed empty. But there was a pool of light in a corner and there was Wright bent over his drawing board. I worried about intruding on art. But my hero was moonlighting, doing floor plans for a local architect—to make ends meet. It was ever thus, I suppose.

Wright's work here begins on page [51] with a cartoon in August of 1961, just after the Berlin Wall was built. And the book ends with the crumbling of the Wall and of communism itself almost thirty years later. The cartoonists had a field day with all of that, partially because, when you're doing floor plans on the side or working at an advertising agency during the day as the caricaturist David Levine was doing, you are free of the elitism, the egoism and the peer pressure of the best and the brightest, the men who saw global conflict as intellectual adventure—chess with real pawns.

My favorite cartoons of that period both made this book. One was a Steve Kelley cartoon in the *San Diego Union* showing Gorbachev and a wife called "Hardliners" tied to chairs with the children "Latvia," "Lithuania" and such running wild around them with slingshots and bows and arrows. She was saying: " 'Spare the rod,' you said . . . 'Give them more freedom,' you said . . . Well, Mr. Perestroika, what now?"

Then there was Mike Peters of the *Dayton Daily News* showing Soviet leaders standing on top of Lenin's tomb with a few new Politburo members—Mickey Mouse and Donald Duck, Superman and Abe Lincoln. "Hold an election, he says," a general is saying. "Let our comrades choose their leaders, he says . . . What could happen? he says . . ." Henry Kissinger or Robert McNamara might find that silly. But it delighted me because I happened to be in Paris when it ran and happened to be walking by a ceremony where Walt Disney executives were cutting a ribbon having to do with the new Euro-Disneyland outside the city. By another coincidence, striking Communist transit workers happened to be demonstrating nearby and they lobbed a couple of eggs and tomatoes at men wearing Mickey and Donald costumes. My first thought was: "At last, the Commies have figured out who their real enemy is."

Thoughts like that rarely make it into learned and footnoted analyses of foreign affairs. But they are at the core of political cartooning. They are the answer to that simplest and most complex of questions: I know what they're saying, but tell me what's really going on?

A Cartoon History of U.S. Foreign Policy is, with no apologies to the White House or State Department, a telling chronicle of what has really gone on in the world since the end of World War II. Like the egg-throwing French Communists, you suddenly get it. The theme of the times, the real story, is laid out right from the start in the work of Joseph Parrish of *The Chicago Tribune,* Dan Dowling of the *New York Herald Tribune,* and Don Hesse of the *St. Louis Globe-Democrat.* That theme, ever valid with Americans, is isolationism versus internationalism. From George Washington on, American instincts have been to avoid foreign entanglements, and because of that internationalists, the best and the brightest, have had to get attention by inflating foreign adversaries into deadly enemies of The American Way of Life—and in the forty-five years covered by this book the chosen enemy was communism. Only cartoonists were equipped to deal with the absurdity of the United States invading Grenada. The U.S. Army had the might to keep reporters and photographers away from their self-defined and self-described triumph, but there is no power on earth capable of turning off the imagination of a cartoonist like Signe Wilkinson of the *San Jose Mercury-News* showing President Ronald Reagan posing with a shotgun and the mounted head of a mouse.

This is great stuff. I read the book while working on one of my own, a history of the presidency of John F. Kennedy. It was helpfully humbling to see, on pages 52 and 53, that Hank Barrow of the *Omaha World-Herald* and Bill Mauldin of the *St. Louis Post-Dispatch* instinctively knew something that statesmen were confused about then and scholars are still debating about now: The "missile gap" that Kennedy used to defeat Richard Nixon in 1960 was a complete and absolute fraud.

I will write about that gap in thousands of words and hundreds of statistics, hoping that readers will get the point and multiple nuances. And I will be admiring and envious of my colleagues at their drawing boards. It's just not fair that their work is so good, that they have the advantage because the cartoon is simply the shortest distance between one point and one citizen. President Lyndon Johnson understood that. He surprised the men around him one morning by smiling after he read a Walter Lippmann column that ripped him up one side and down the other.

"Why are you smiling, Mr. President?" said the least timid of his men.

"I'm glad Lippmann can't draw," said the president.

Richard Reeves

Sag Harbor, N.Y.
September 12, 1990

★★ A Cartoon History of ★★

United States
Foreign Policy

★★ From 1945 to the Present ★★

1

One World into Two: The Beginning of the Cold War

On August 6, 1945, as the aircraft *Enola Gay* headed for Hiroshima bearing the atomic bomb "Little Boy," its commander warned the crew over the intercom: "This is history, so watch your language." The resulting blasts from that bomb and a second dropped at Nagasaki three days later killed more than 200,000 people and leveled the two Japanese cities. As President Harry S Truman had hoped, the United States' use of its atomic bomb brought World War II to a quick close: Japan surrendered within the week, on August 15, and the victorious Allies—the United States, Britain, France, and the Soviet Union—were left with the task of rebuilding a ravaged world in the shadow of the nuclear weapon.

Journey's End - 1945

Daniel R. Fitzpatrick. St. Louis Post-Dispatch.

And Company Already Arriving

Jay N. Darling. From *Ding's Half Century*, John M. Henry, ed. New York, Duell, Sloan & Pearce, 1962. J.N. ("Ding") Darling Foundation, Fleming Building, Des Moines, Iowa.

The Speaker's Platform

Edwin Marcus. Copyright © 1949 by The New York Times Company. Reprinted by permission.

Determined to avoid the mistakes that had doomed President Woodrow Wilson's efforts to create a League of Nations after World War I, the Big Four had begun planning in 1943 for a new and effective world organization to keep the peace. This time, in contrast to Wilson's 1919 experience, both House and Senate by wide margins supported the idea of committing the United States to such an organization. When representatives of forty-six nations (including a U.S. delegation of both Democrats and Republicans) met in San Francisco in April 1945, they were determined to succeed. Despite some strong criticism at home, the Senate overwhelmingly approved the UN Charter on July 28, 1945. To optimists it looked as if the United States, with its vibrant economy and democratic ideals, in cooperation with its powerful Soviet ally, could help ensure a peaceful future for a unified world.

Planning the Dinner

Cloyd Sweigert. Copyright © San Francisco Chronicle. Reprinted by permission.

But hopes for "one world" soon evaporated. The friendship between the United States and Soviet leader "Uncle Joe" Stalin did not last twelve months after Hitler's defeat. The position of the Allied armies in Europe at the end of the war placed the USSR squarely in control of Eastern Europe. Between 1945 and 1948 Moscow consolidated its position in a series of rigged elections that converted Bulgaria, Hungary, Poland, and Romania to "people's democracies" under tight Soviet control. An "iron curtain" had descended across the Continent, former British prime minister Winston Churchill warned in 1946.

Meanwhile, the United States demobilized as rapidly as it could, in response to the "I-Wanna-Go-Home" demonstrations by U.S. troops in Europe backed up

Great Expectations

Edwin Marcus. Copyright © 1947 by The New York Times Company. Reprinted by permission.

by vocal "Bring-Daddy-Back-Home" clubs in the United States. West European countries tottered on the brink of economic and political collapse and Western Communist parties, taking their cues from Moscow, began making significant electoral headway in the chaos. When a war-exhausted Britain admitted that it could no longer help keep order in the eastern Mediterranean, President Truman proclaimed the doctrine that bears his name, pledging to "support free peoples who are resisting attempted subjugation by armed minorities or by outside pressures."

The Marshall Plan, which provided thirteen billion dollars to sixteen European countries between 1948 and 1951, reflected the American belief that prosperity

King Canute Makes a Clean Sweep of It

Cal Alley. Reprinted by permission of The Commercial Appeal (Memphis).

Some Day They'll Come Crawling Back to Her

Joseph Parrish. Chicago Tribune. Reprinted by permission.

would ensure peace and democracy by preventing, in Truman's words, the "seeds of totalitarian regimes" from being "nurtured by misery and want." Critics dubbed the plan Operation Rathole and objected that "Uncle Santa Claus" should concentrate on American problems.

There are Such

Talburt. World Journal Tribune (New York).

Another Light Goes Out

Tom Little. The Nashville Tennessean.

When democracy in Czechoslovakia came to an abrupt end in 1948, congressional alarm in the United States was strong enough to overcome the traditional American fear of "entangling alliances." In June a bipartisan majority approved the Vandenberg Resolution that paved the way for the formation of the North

Unintentional Cupid

Richard Q. Yardley. The Baltimore Sun.

Atlantic Treaty Organization (NATO) a year later. The same month, U.S.–Soviet differences came to a head over Berlin. Originally divided among the four victorious Allies at the end of the war, as was all of Germany, Berlin became a two-part city with the onset of the Cold War. Soviet resentment of the Marshall Plan and West Berlin's increasing integration into the Western bloc led Moscow

Nobody is Happy

Burt R. Thomas. Reprinted with permission from The Detroit News, a Gannett newspaper, 1949.

No Pushover

Fred O. Seibel. Richmond Times-Dispatch.

Jumping-Off Place

Joseph Parrish. Chicago Tribune.

to blockade the Western sector in June 1948. The United States responded with an airlift—Operation Vittles—of 4500 tons of food and supplies a week that kept two and a half million people alive for eleven months. The blockade was lifted in May 1949, within weeks of the signing of the NATO treaty, but it would not be the last time the Berlin issue threatened to drag the superpowers into a shooting war. That prospect grew more ominous when the Soviets broke the United States' nuclear monopoly by exploding their own atomic bomb in 1949.

Rude Awakening

Vaughn Shoemaker. Chicago Daily News.

2

Containment in the East

While the United States and its allies were securing their European flank, a major upheaval was under way on the far side of the globe. China was in the

Wait Till He Gets to the Next Stall

Dan Dowling. World Journal Tribune/New York Herald Tribune.

throes of a long civil war between Chiang Kai-shek's Nationalist government and Mao Zedong's Communists. The United States supported Chiang, but Washington underestimated Mao's strength and the degree to which the inefficiency and corruption of the Chiang government had undermined its support among the Chinese people.

Despite American diplomatic efforts and some two billion dollars in aid and

How Long?

Paule Loring. The Evening Bulletin (Providence), 1949.

Been to the Cleaners

Tom Little. The Nashville Tennessean.

military supplies to the Nationalist government between 1945 and 1949, Chiang was driven off the mainland in 1949 and fled to the offshore island of Formosa (the Japanese name for Taiwan). A fierce domestic fight ensued in Washington over who had ''lost'' China. A white paper issued by the State Department in 1949 placed the blame squarely on Chiang, but many felt the United States had not done nearly enough to prevent China's more than a half-billion people from falling into the Communist camp—which meant the Soviet camp in the view of the State Department: "The Peiping government may be a colonial Russian government. . . . It is not the Government of China. It does not pass the first test. It is not Chinese." The United States refused to recognize the new People's Republic of China (PRC) and blocked its entry into the UN.

Hard to Recognize

Burt R. Thomas. Reprinted with permission from The Detroit News, a Gannett newspaper, 1949.

In June 1950, only months after the Communist victory in China, some 75,000 Communist North Korean troops crossed the Thirty-eighth Parallel, the dividing line between North and South Korea, and quickly overran the South Korean capital of Seoul. The United States immediately blamed Moscow. The following day the UN Security Council condemned North Korea's aggression

"Oh, We Recognize You All Right."

Ed Holland. Chicago Tribune.

and voted that UN members should "render every assistance" in restoring the peace. The Soviet Union missed its chance to veto the UN action because it was boycotting council proceedings as a result of the UN's refusal to seat the PRC.

For the next thirty-seven months the United States provided 90 percent of the UN forces, initially under the command of U.S. general Douglas MacArthur. The war went badly for the UN forces at first, but when the tide turned and the North Korean troops were pushed back across the Thirty-eighth Parallel, MacArthur received permission from the UN General Assembly to pursue the fighting on the North Korean side of the border. Ignoring warnings from the Communist

Starting Something?

Edwin Marcus. Copyright 1950 by The New York Times Company. Reprinted with permission.

Not Much Help, But It's Nice to Have Company

Jensen. Chicago Daily News.

Chinese that Beijing would not stand idly by during an invasion of North Korea, MacArthur led the attack to the Chinese border along the Yalu River. He turned what was nearly a victory into a rout as some 200,000 Communist Chinese troops intervened to turn back the UN forces. MacArthur believed "There is no substitute for victory" and was prepared to risk nuclear war with the Chinese. Truman preferred caution, and the disagreement culminated in his firing MacArthur for insubordination in 1951. Although the general was welcomed home to ticker-tape parades, the view eventually prevailed that if he had had his way and pursued a full-scale war with the Chinese, it would have been "the wrong war, at the wrong place, at the wrong time, and with the wrong enemy," in the words of Gen. Omar Bradley, then head of the Joint Chiefs of Staff.

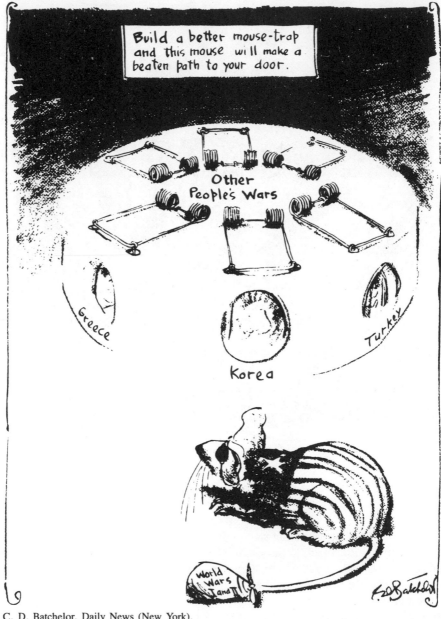

C. D. Batchelor. Daily News (New York).

Repair in the Wall

PACIFIC

AID PACT WITH JAPAN

DEFENSE

Don Hesse. St. Louis Globe-Democrat.

With the loss of its ally in China and the hostilities in Korea, the United States modified its plans for vanquished Japan. Under the terms of Japan's 1947 constitution, dictated by the United States, the country pledged not to maintain military forces. But after the outbreak of the Korean War, Washington ordered Japan to set up a national police reserve as a paramilitary force. The United States signed a peace treaty with Japan in 1951 and, four years later, an aid agreement.

Korea and China figured heavily in the election of 1952, in which the Democrats lost to Republican candidate Gen. Dwight D. Eisenhower, who had commanded the Allied forces in Europe during World War II. The popular Ike

"And the Best Part is that *He's* Paying *Us* for the Ride."

Bill Mauldin. Reprinted with special permission of North America Syndicate, Inc.

won in a landslide. His secretary of state, John Foster Dulles, was a man obsessed with the containment of communism. By the end of Dulles' tenure in 1959, the United States was a member of some forty security arrangements linking it with nations strategically located to block Soviet expansion. These included the Southeast Asian Treaty Organization (SEATO), whose specific aim was to deter the PRC from spreading communism to Indochina. The Eisenhower administration also provided Chiang's government on Taiwan roughly $250 million a year. The two governments signed a mutual defense pact in 1954.

The Chinese Nationalists, who throughout the 1950s attempted to regain control of the mainland, launched repeated raids from the tiny islands of Quemoy and Matsu, several miles offshore. When Beijing responded in 1954 and 1955 by shelling the islands and pledging to "liberate" Taiwan, the United States passed

Quite a Pot Building up.

Scott Long. The Minneapolis Tribune. Reprinted with permission of the Star Tribune.

the Formosa Resolution, giving Eisenhower authority to use troops, if necessary, to defend Formosa. That crisis was defused but resurfaced in 1958, by which time the United States had installed nuclear-capable missiles on Taiwan. At the very brink of nuclear war both sides backed down. The United States promised

Hugh Haynie. Reprinted by permission of The Greensboro Daily News (North Carolina).

to defend Quemoy and Matsu from the Communists, who agreed to stop the shelling, in return for which the Nationalists renounced the future use of force to regain the mainland.

The Line is Drawn

John Fischetti. Copyright © Newspaper Enterprise Association, Inc.

3

Decolonization

The disintegration of the old imperial system transformed the postwar world. Between 1946 and 1960 thirty-seven new nations were created from the colonial empires of Western countries. The United States gave its only colony, the Philippines, independence in 1946 and began pressing its European allies to do the same for theirs.

The developing nations became the new battleground between communism and capitalism, with aid and trade major weapons. The stakes were high: the Third World was rich in raw materials on which the industrialized nations depended.

To help developing nations around the world help themselves, Truman announced a "bold new program" called Point 4 in his 1949 inaugural address. The idea was that U.S. technical know-how could help reduce poverty in the underdeveloped world and make countries less vulnerable to the appeal of communism. Truman preferred, in historian Thomas A. Bailey's words, "to

Twentieth Century Dilemma

Scott Long. The Minneapolis Tribune. Reprinted with permission of the Star Tribune.

Couldn't Do Better with a Hammer and Sickle!

Herbert L. Block. Copyright 1950 by Herblock in The Washington Post.

spend millions to prevent people from becoming Communists rather than spend billions to shoot them after they became Communists.''

Eisenhower also saw foreign aid as an effective anti-Communist weapon, but he emphasized trade and military support rather than economic aid. This not only helped him balance the U.S. federal budget but also reduced congressional opposition to the foreign aid program.

"The Lamb is Still There. It's Just Been Integrated."

Herbert L. Block. Copyright 1953 by Herblock in The Washington Post.

American largesse was not always appreciated, however, even in Latin America, which received large infusions of U.S. aid. In 1954, after the Central Intelligence Agency (CIA) helped overthrow the leftist leader of Guatemala, Col. Jácobo Arbenz Guzmán, who had nationalized extensive property belonging to the U.S.-owned United Fruit Company, there was an outburst of anti-Americanism.

The House that "Jack" Built

Art Sloggatt. New York Mirror.

Demonstration on Filling a Vacuum

John R. Stampone. Reprint courtesy of *Army Times*. Copyright by Times Journal Publishing Company, Springfield, Virginia.

The depth of "anti-Yank" sentiment south of the border was brought home by the violently hostile reaction when Vice President Richard M. Nixon made a goodwill tour to Latin America in 1958.

Meanwhile, in the Middle East waning colonialism and growing nationalism were creating a power vacuum. The United States was afraid the Soviet Union might be tempted to fill it, jeopardizing Western access to the region's oil and to the vital Suez Canal. Here too the CIA went into action. The United States helped overthrow the leftist government of Mohammad Mossadeq, who took power in Iran in 1953 and nationalized British-owned oil refineries, and helped return the pro-American Shah Mohammad Reza Pahlavi to the Peacock Throne. At American urging Turkey, Iran, Iraq, Pakistan, and Britain in 1955 formed the Baghdad Pact to guard the region against Communist inroads.

An Increasingly Difficult Neighborhood

Dan Dowling. World Journal Tribune/New York Herald Tribune. Field Newspaper Syndicate.

"Cross My Palms with Silver."

Thiele in the Los Angeles Mirror-News.

"You Fellows aren't Going to Put it Back Just like That, are You?"

Herbert L. Block. Copyright 1957 by Herblock in The Washington Post.

In Egypt, the United States and Britain were planning a seventy-million-dollar kickoff grant for a high dam at Aswan on the upper Nile River, a project estimated to increase Egypt's arable lands by 25 percent. But Egyptian president Gamal Abdel Nasser was also flirting with the Communists: he recognized the People's Republic of China and signed an arms agreement with Czechoslovakia in 1955. Dulles withdrew from the dam plan in July 1956 to punish Nasser for playing both sides, a move that backfired when Nasser retaliated by closing the Suez Canal.

"Well, It's Sort of New with Us"

Herbert L. Block. Copyright 1957 by Herblock in The Washington Post.

The resulting Suez crisis pitted the United States against two of its closest allies, Britain and France—who, without consulting Washington, carried out a joint military operation with Israel in October 1956 to regain control of the canal. In the face of pressure from the United States and the UN, the invading troops were forced to pull out.

Nasser's rapprochement with the Soviet Union after the United States withdrew its Aswan dam aid offer was viewed in Washington as ominous. The administration's answer was the Eisenhower Doctrine of 1957, which promised U.S. troops to any Middle Eastern government that asked for help in repelling Communist aggression. Eisenhower did briefly dispatch the marines to Lebanon the following year (although he did not invoke the doctrine), but the civil strife in that country continued after the marines' departure. This seemed to underscore the limitations of a foreign policy predicated on a strict Communist-versus-Free World reading of world events.

Birth pangs for nations south of the Sahara were particularly severe, since most were poorly prepared. Belgium abandoned its huge colony in the Congo in

Robert Bastian. Copyright © San Francisco Chronicle. Reprinted by permission.

Heating the Branding Irons.

Art Poinier. Reprinted with permission from The Detroit News, a Gannett newspaper, copyright © 1961.

1960 in the midst of anticolonial riots. Civil war ensued as the resource-rich Katanga province tried to secede. Although the USSR initially backed the central government of Patrice Lumumba, hoping to get the Congo into the Communist camp, Moscow lost interest in intervention after Lumumba was murdered in 1961. Over the objections of the Soviet Union, which refused to pay its share of the costs, the UN sent troops—which succeeded in putting down the insurrection in 1962.

Ranan Lurie. Cartoonews International.

In Africa, as in other places, the dominant issue was not communism or capitalism. For Africans it was color and colonialism, and between 1955 and 1965 much of sub-Saharan Africa threw off its white colonial rulers. Portugal hung onto its colonies in Angola and Mozambique for another draining decade before it pulled out, leaving a new ring of "front-line states" to face the last white minority governments: Rhodesia (which became Zimbabwe under black rule in 1980) and South Africa. By 1988, only South Africa and its colony of

H. Clay Bennett. Reprinted from the St. Petersburg (Fla.) Times.

Namibia, which it occupied illegally, remained under white minority rule and were the site of continuing turmoil. South Africa's practice of apartheid—strict racial separation and brutally enforced legal discrimination—made it a pariah state, but it still showed no sign of willingness to turn power over to the black majority.

4

The Cold War Heats up

By 1953 both superpowers had exploded thermonuclear weapons that dwarfed the explosive power of the bombs dropped on Hiroshima and Nagasaki. The contestants were off and running: the United States to try maintaining its lead and the USSR to try catching up.

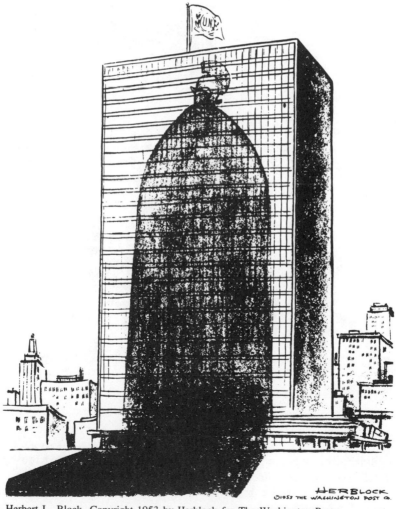

Herbert L. Block. Copyright 1953 by Herblock for The Washington Post.

The year also saw the death of Joseph Stalin. The changing of the guard in the Kremlin led to a switch from saber-rattling to a "peace offensive." Although many were skeptical, the fresh wind from Moscow led to an outbreak of "summit fever" in the United States, and in 1955 (over conservative protests) Eisenhower met Nikita Khrushchev, who was then rapidly rising to the top of the Communist party pecking order, in Geneva. But the warmer "spirit of Geneva"

But How About the Basic Design!

John Milt Morris. AP Newsfeatures, 1953.

generated by the meeting did not last long: little of substance was accomplished, and the differences between the superpowers remained great. As Khrushchev pointed out, "If anybody thinks we shall forget about Marx, Engels and Lenin, he is mistaken." There was a brief thaw, but the cold war was far from over.

At home, President Eisenhower was preoccupied with balancing the budget.

The Cheshire Cat

"THIS TIME IT VANISHED QUITE SLOWLY, BEGINNING WITH THE END OF THE TAIL, AND ENDING WITH THE GRIN, WHICH REMAINED SOME TIME AFTER THE REST OF IT HAD GONE." (Alice In Wonderland)

Scott Long. The Minneapolis Tribune. Reprinted with permission of Star Tribune.

Mort Walker. Reprinted with special permission of King Features Syndicate, Inc.

Marked Man

Art Bimrose. Reprinted by permission of The Portland Oregonian.

Relying more heavily on nuclear weapons, which provided greater "bang for the buck," than on conventional forces seemed to provide a way to cut expenses in defense secretary Charles E. Wilson's Pentagon. Defense spending had ballooned during the Korean War. The United States therefore adopted the policy of "massive retaliation," confident in its ability to deter war and defend U.S. allies in Western Europe and elsewhere by threatening to respond to any attack with nuclear weapons. Although the Soviets had exploded their own H-bomb, they still lacked the bombers that could get the weapons to their targets and return home again.

Superpower relations were plunged back into the deep freeze after Soviet troops put a brutal end to an uprising in Hungary in 1956. Washington condemned the action but, reluctant to risk nuclear war to help the Hungarians, remained on the sidelines.

The following year the Soviet Union punctured American self-confidence with the successful firing of the first intercontinental ballistic missile, a coup it quickly followed by putting Sputnik—the first man-made satellite—into orbit. The Soviets had demonstrated that they could now hit any point they wanted to in the United States, a consideration that made the prospect of massive retaliation a two-way street.

"Ten, Nine, Eight, Seven..."

John Fischetti. Copyright © 1957 Newspaper Enterprise Association, Inc.

"Are You Tryin' to Start a War?"

John Fischetti. Copyright © 1958 Newspaper Enterprise Association, Inc.

The Soviets took advantage of their new nuclear clout in the fall of 1958, turning up the flame under the volatile issue of Berlin, which was still divided into Soviet and Western sectors. West Berlin, located inside East Germany 110 miles from the border with West Germany, was a bone in Khrushchev's throat—an all-too-visible reminder of West Germany's growing prosperity and a base for anti-Communist propaganda and espionage. Some three million East German refugees, many of them skilled, had fled to West Germany since 1949. The West had never recognized the Soviet-dominated German Democratic Republic, and had increasingly integrated the Federal Republic of Germany into Western defenses and markets.

In November 1958, Khrushchev proposed making Berlin a free city. If the West did not agree and remove its troops within six months, he would turn East Berlin over to Communist East German control, at which point the Western allies

"Next Month? Why Yes, I Think I Might be Able to..."

Herbert L. Block. Copyright 1959 by Herblock for The Washington Post.

Mountains Out of Mole Hills

Cal Alley. Reprinted by permission of The Commercial Appeal (Memphis).

Bill Mauldin. Reprinted with special permission of North America Syndicate, Inc.

would either have to give up control of West Berlin or fight for it. The Cold War had never before been quite so close to turning hot, but the United States called Khrushchev's bluff and stood firm. Khrushchev, apparently more interested in talking than fighting, let the six-month ultimatum expire quietly when Eisenhower agreed to a summit meeting. The two leaders met, over the vehement opposition of conservatives, at Camp David, the presidential retreat in Maryland, in September 1959.

Chas. O. Bissell. Reprinted courtesy of The Nashville Tennessean.

Camp David only temporarily defused the Berlin situation: the two countries' positions were too far apart. A four-power summit was planned for May 1960, but the shooting down of an American U-2 spy plane over Soviet territory two weeks before the summit was to take place in Paris torpedoed it. Although the United States badly bungled its handling of the incident, Khrushchev squandered any diplomatic points he might have gained at U.S. expense by his boorish behavior at the UN General Assembly in New York the following fall. After shouting and hurling insults, he removed his shoe and banged it on the desk in front of him, disgusting many of the delegates whose governments he was trying to woo.

In June 1961 Khrushchev again threatened to turn Berlin over to the East Germans unless the Western nations recognized East German sovereignty. Just over a month later Moscow cut off the growing hemorrhage of East Germans to

"See How Many are Staying on Our Side."

Don Wright. Reprinted by permission: Tribune Media Services.

Missile Gap.

Bill Mauldin. Reprinted with special permission of North America Syndicate, Inc.

the West by putting up the Berlin Wall. European and American critics were outraged by the lack of response from the United States, but Washington was unwilling to risk nuclear war.

In the meantime, the United States and the Soviet Union continued their nuclear tests: by 1958 there was a nuclear test in the atmosphere almost every four days, and public pressure to call them off was mounting along with the evidence that the resulting nuclear fallout was harmful to people and the environment. But in the political atmosphere of the late 1950s there was little prospect that such an agreement could be reached. Instead, the arms race continued to gain speed.

John F. Kennedy's campaign rhetoric in 1960 focused on a dangerous "missile gap" that had opened between the United States and the Soviet Union. Although

"Now This is the Gissile Map, I Mean Gappile Miss, I Mean..."

Hank Barrow. Reprinted by permission of the Omaha World-Herald.

it turned out that the gap actually favored the United States, Kennedy increased the defense budget for both nuclear and conventional weapons. The Soviets in turn resumed nuclear testing in 1961, after a three-year unilateral moratorium, and the United States quickly followed suit.

"I'd Better Take a Second Look at That Lock!"

L.D. Warren. Reprinted by permission of The Cincinnati Enquirer.

High Noon

Bill Crawford. Copyright © 1961 Newspaper Enterprise Association, Inc.

The world entered upon the most dangerous period of the Cold War in October 1962 with the U.S. discovery that the Soviet Union was installing nuclear-armed medium-range missiles in Cuba. The island, ninety miles off Florida's coast, had been under the control of Kremlin ally Fidel Castro since 1959. An earlier attempt to remove the dictator, the CIA-assisted Bay of Pigs invasion (which led to the CIA being dubbed the Cuban Invasion Authority), had ended in disaster and embarrassment for the Kennedy administration. This time, Kennedy would not back down: he insisted that Khrushchev remove the missiles. The world watched nervously as the two sides moved closer than ever before to nuclear war.

Eyeball to eyeball, as Secretary of State Dean Rusk put it, Khrushchev blinked, and Moscow and Washington decided it was time to ensure that such a crisis would never recur. Despite conservative opposition in the United States,

Retreat

Hy Rosen. Copyright © 1962 by Hy Rosen, The Times-Union (Albany, N.Y.).

the two countries signed the Limited Test Ban Treaty (prohibiting nuclear explosions in the atmosphere, outer space, and under water) in 1963 and the "hot line" accord that set up rapid, reliable communication between Washington and Moscow.

"It's Not Practical—There's No Assurance that It Wouldn't Also Save the Russians."

Herbert L. Block. Copyright © 1963 by Herblock for The Washington Post.

5

Allies and Adversaries

The Soviet Union's growing nuclear strength was placing serious strains on the Atlantic Alliance, by then in its troublesome teens. To many Europeans, Washington's claim that it would defend them with nuclear weapons against a Soviet attack no longer looked very believable. American inability or unwillingness

"The Door was Too Small—I Had to Blast."

John Fischetti. Copyright © 1960 Newspaper Enterprise Association, Inc.

"...But I was About to Ask *You* to Give *Me* a Hand!"

Charles Brooks. Reprinted by permission of The Birmingham News.

"French Impressionism, I Guess."

Bil Canfield. Newark News. Reprinted by permission.

to prevent the Soviets from crushing the Hungarian rebellion or erecting the Berlin Wall was seen by some Europeans as proof that the United States could not be counted on to trade "Chicago for Hamburg" if war broke out in Europe.

Britain and France therefore elected to build their own nuclear deterrents. This galled the United States, which would have far preferred its allies to help field more of the ground forces in Europe than spend their money on what Washington saw as redundant nuclear forces. The growing British and French nuclear strength, combined with West Germany's insistence on more say over nuclear strategy, also threatened the U.S. leadership role in NATO, damaged in any case by Soviet nuclear successes. The Kennedy administration tried to reassert Washington's leadership and to stop the further spread of nuclear forces by proposing a multilateral nuclear force (consisting of U.S. nuclear weapons under Allied control), but those efforts led to more friction, and the scheme was abandoned by the Johnson administration.

French president Charles de Gaulle's doubts about the reliability of the United States as an ally meshed nicely with his ambitions to rebuild France into a global power. The United States had encouraged its European allies to take steps toward

"I'm Here, Ludwig . . . Have No Fear!"

Pierre Bellocq (Peb). From The Philadelphia Inquirer. Reprinted with permission.

"Before We Take You into Our Club

Robert Bastian. Copyright © 1967 San Francisco Chronicle. Reprinted by permission.

economic integration and defense cooperation, but de Gaulle had his own ideas for a French-led continent, independent of the United States. He blocked Britain's attempts to join the European Community, or Common Market, in 1963, 1967, and 1968 (Britain was finally admitted in 1973). Moreover, after earlier withdrawing some French troops from the NATO command, de Gaulle removed the rest of them in July 1966 and announced that foreign troops would not be welcome on French soil after April 1967.

The Adamant Concierge

Richard Q. Yardley. The Baltimore Sun.

"If You Won't Play My Way I'll Take My Ball and Go Home."

Hugh Haynie. Copyright © Courier-Journal, Louisville Times Co. Reprinted with permission.

But—A Communist is a Communist is a Communist

L.D. Warren. Reprinted by permission of The Cincinnati Enquirer.

While NATO allies squabbled, members of the Communist bloc on the other side of the Iron Curtain were having problems of their own. Yugoslav leader Tito had broken with Moscow in 1948 and, even though he had patched up the quarrel in 1956, continued his independent policies. Khrushchev's denunciation of Stalin's abuses during a "secret speech" before the 1956 Communist Party

Internal Trouble

Edwin Marcus. Copyright © 1948 by The New York Times Company. Reprinted with permission.

Congress signaled some loosening of authoritarianism inside the Soviet Union, which had unexpected repercussions. Within months, people took to the streets to protest harsh dictatorial rule, first in Poland and then in Hungary, where demonstrations quickly grew into a large-scale revolt that ended only when Moscow sent in Soviet troops.

"I'll be Glad to Restore Peace to the Middle East, Too."

Herbert L. Block. Copyright 1956 by Herblock for The Washington Post.

Two Diggers—One Headstone

Cal Alley. Reprinted by permission of The Commercial Appeal (Memphis).

Robert Bastian. Copyright San Francisco Chronicle. Reprinted by permission.

Soviet relations with fellow-Communist giant China were rapidly souring. Mao disapproved of Khrushchev's variations on Leninism and charged the Soviet leader with "coddling" the capitalist West. The two were also competing for influence in Asia and Africa. The rift between Beijing and Moscow grew wider and deeper, and in 1960 Moscow called home its technicians and scientists and suspended its assistance to China's nuclear program. China nevertheless succeeded on its own in building a nuclear device and joined the ranks of the nuclear powers in 1964 the day Khrushchev was removed from power in the Kremlin. China's campaign to win allies was less successful than its nuclear program, however. Even its staunchest Asian friend, Sukarno of Indonesia, was thrown out of power in 1965.

"Ever Occur to You, We May be Doing Something Wrong?"

Bil Canfield, Newark News. Reprinted by permission.

"... Drunk? ... Of Course I'm Not Drunk!!"

Paul Conrad. Copyright © 1965 Los Angeles Times Syndicate. Reprinted by permission.

6

Vietnam

Despite communism's setbacks and a return to peace in Korea, Washington continued to be wary of Beijing's and Moscow's continuing attempts to export Marxism–Leninism to developing nations in Asia. Where possible, Washington

Another Hole in the Dike

Fred Q. Seibel. Richmond Times-Dispatch. Reprinted with permission.

Just Leaned on It a Little . . .

Karl Hubenthal. Los Angeles Herald Examiner.

relied on its European allies who still held colonies to stave off revolutions that might end in Communist victories.

When France, whose empire at the end of World War II included Indochina, was defeated in 1954 at Dienbienphu by Ho Chi Minh's Communist-supported

"May I Speak to Our Staunch, Loyal Ally, the Head of the Vietnamese Government—Whoever It is Today."

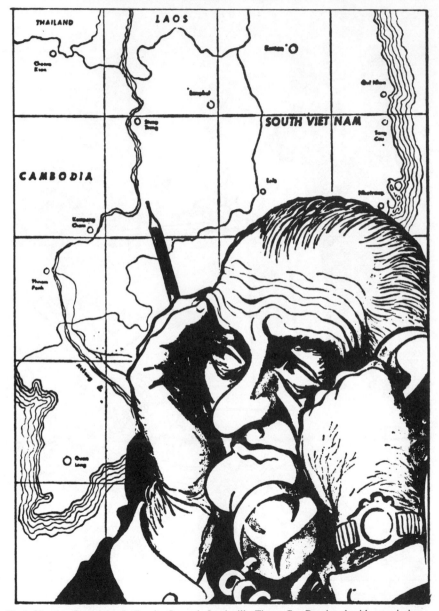

Hugh Haynie. Copyright © Courier-Journal, Louisville Times Co. Reprinted with permission.

The Strategists

Bill Mauldin. Reprinted with special permission of North America Syndicate, Inc.

forces, Vietnam was divided into two countries, with Ho in control of the north. Eisenhower worried that if the southern half fell to communism it would, like a falling domino, take neighboring countries with it.

Washington therefore began sending aid to the South Vietnamese government of Ngo Dinh Diem and his armed forces. The North Vietnamese, meanwhile,

"Those Kids are Just Plain Irresponsible."

John Fischetti. New York Herald Tribune, Inc.

were happy to accept help from both Moscow and Beijing. Kennedy increased economic support for South Vietnam and quintupled the number of U.S. military "advisers," but before his assassination in 1963 he began having doubts about the ability of Diem, whose government was corrupt and unpopular, to rally his country. With U.S. support, Diem was ousted. Saigon subsequently went through a succession of unstable governments. Although Kennedy's successor

"Name a Clean One."

Herbert L. Block. Copyright 1965 by Herblock for The Washington Post.

"Happy Birthday to Youuu . . . Happy Birthday to . . ."

Wayne Stayskal. Reprinted by permission: Tribune Media Services.

"Could You Point Out the Ground You've Taken? We're Here to Secure and Develop It Economically."

Pat Oliphant. Copyright © 1966 Universal Press Syndicate. Reprinted with permission. All rights reserved.

Lyndon Johnson called the survival of the South Vietnamese government essential to U.S. national security and committed more and more troops, it became less and less clear to Americans who or what they were defending.

Pictures of the conflict in Vietnam, the first televised war, became a daily staple in American living rooms for ten years, and the experience deeply divided the American people. Although dissent against Johnson's policy of "Americanizing" the war was relatively small at first, it reached overwhelming proportions by the end of the decade, as the war continued to go badly despite increasing amounts of economic aid, fresh troops (eighteen-year-olds began being drafted to fight in 1968), and supplies. The Saigon government's control of the countryside was so weak that villages it took during the day were reoccupied by the Vietcong the same night. One casualty of the war was LBJ himself, who in 1968 surprised the country by deciding not to run for the presidency a second time.

Drawing by David Levine. Reprinted with permission from The New York Review of Books. Copyright 1966 NYREV, INC.

Johnson's successor, Richard M. Nixon, ran on a pledge to end the war. He hoped to achieve "peace with honor" in Vietnam, getting Americans out without creating doubts among U.S. allies about this country's reliability as a friend. He planned to do so by the gradual "Vietnamization" of the war, training Saigon to fight its own battles.

"Now, About the Chairs!"

Cal Alley. Reprinted by permission of The Commercial Appeal (Memphis).

"I Never Did Say How, but I Told You I'd Get You Out of Vietnam."

John Fischetti. Chicago Daily News, 1970.

Meanwhile, as delegates to the peace talks in Paris squabbled interminably over the shape of the negotiating table, the war was escalating. Nixon secretly ordered the bombing of Cambodia in 1969. American troops invaded Cambodia in April 1970 to help prop up a pro-American general, Lon Nol, against the

"Now Here's My Plan For Getting Out of the World with Honor."

Tom Darcy. Newsday (New York). Reprinted by permission.

Paul Szep. Reprinted courtesy of The Boston Globe.

Cambodian Communists (the Khmer Rouge) and to prevent the North Vietnamese from staging attacks on the south from Cambodian territory. News of the invasion led to further intensification of the antiwar protest movement. Fighting in Laos would escalate, too, before American troops left Southeast Asia.

Nixon did finally withdraw American troops, in 1973. The tottering South Vietnamese government they left behind did not hold out long: Saigon was overrun by the Vietcong in 1975, and Americans at home watched their television screens as the last Americans escaped the country by helicopter from the roof of the American embassy in Saigon. The war was finally over, but it left wounds on the American psyche that would take a long time to heal.

Jules Feiffer. Copyright © 1972 Jules Feiffer. Reprinted with permission Universal Press Syndicate. All rights reserved.

7

President vs. Congress

The long war in Southeast Asia sparked major political skirmishes back in Washington. An early blowup between Johnson and Congress was set off by the Gulf of Tonkin Resolution, which in 1964 gave the President the go-ahead to

"Only Thing We're Sure of—There is a Tonkin Gulf!"

Bil Canfield. Newark Star-Ledger. Reprinted with permission.

"For Political Reasons, We Should Spare Hanoi, Haiphong and the Senate Foreign Relations Committee..."

Robinson in The Indianapolis News. Reprinted by permission.

"You Don't Just Walk into the Oval Office . . ."

John W. Dean III. Draper Hill. Copyright © 1973, Draper Hill, in The Commercial Appeal (Memphis).

send combat troops to Vietnam without an actual declaration of war. Four years later, it emerged that the administration, in alleging that the U.S. destroyer *Maddox* had been attacked in the Gulf, had misrepresented the circumstances. Congress repealed the resolution in 1970, in the midst of the heat generated by Nixon's invasion of Cambodia.

Richard Nixon was a man who did not trust large bureaucracies. Much of what he and his national security adviser (and later secretary of state) Henry A. Kissinger did in Southeast Asia (like the secret bombing of Cambodia) was accomplished by bypassing normal foreign policy procedures. Decisions were made in the White House and executed through secret back channels, including CIA-run covert operations, leaving State Department personnel and Congress in the dark.

"Go Forth and Infiltrate?"

Paul Szep. Reprinted courtesy of The Boston Globe.

Supreme Showdown

Jim Dobbins in Boston Herald-Examiner.

Bill Sanders. Reprinted with special permission of North America Syndicate, Inc.

The CIA's role in carrying out Nixon's foreign policy agenda became clearer to the American public as the details of the President's connection with the 1972 break-in at Democratic party headquarters at the Watergate were revealed. While Nixon's role in the affair was investigated, Congress reined in the President by passing the War Powers Act and appointed commissions to investigate CIA abuses at home and abroad. Details of the CIA's involvement in a number of assassination attempts on foreign leaders and its role in the overthrow of Chilean socialist president Salvador Allende Gossens became public, as did an illegal intelligence operation directed against American antiwar activists.

Increasingly preoccupied by the Watergate mess, much of it documented by secret tapes of presidential conversations, Nixon turned more and more of the

Tony Auth. Philadelphia Inquirer. Copyright © 1974. Reprinted with permission of Universal Press Syndicate. All rights reserved.

responsibility for foreign policymaking over to Kissinger. Nixon chose in 1974 to resign rather than be impeached. Although Congress seemed to have won the day, the overall image of the United States abroad had been weakened by the collapse of the Nixon presidency.

"Will the Last One Indicted Please Put the Lights Out?"

John Fischetti. Chicago Daily News.

8

Détente

The war in Vietnam had already tarnished the U.S. image abroad by the time Nixon took office in 1969. In addition, the Soviet Union had by that time nearly caught up with the United States in the nuclear arms race. But the backlash

"It's Just a Business Call. We Want to Let You Know that We are Around in Case of Need."

Ed Valtman. Hartford Times (Conn.). Rothco.

"Turn up the Cloud Machine, Angels Enter from the Left—"

Don Wright. Reprinted by permission: Tribune Media Services.

against the war at home was creating pressures for the United States to cut defense spending. How, then, to reassert U.S. influence in the world?

The Nixon–Kissinger answer was détente, a lessening of tensions, with the Soviet Union. The idea was to use common U.S.–Soviet interests—particularly in arms control—as the cornerstone in building "mutually advantageous" relationships between the two superpowers. By giving the Soviets a stake in the status quo, for example through lucrative trading arrangements like the 1975 grain deal (which was vehemently opposed by conservatives), Washington hoped to discourage Moscow from stirring up trouble in the Third World in order to spread communism.

Détente's most visible product was SALT I. The first strategic arms limitation

Jeff MacNelly. Reprinted by permission: Tribune Media Services.

talks (SALT I) led to a treaty signed in 1972 that limited offensive arms and defensive antiballistic missile (ABM) weapons. But critics were quick to note that SALT I and the Vladivostok accord, signed by Leonid I. Brezhnev and Gerald R. Ford two years later, capped but did not reverse the arms race and left a number of unsolved problems.

"Yours Looks Nice Too"

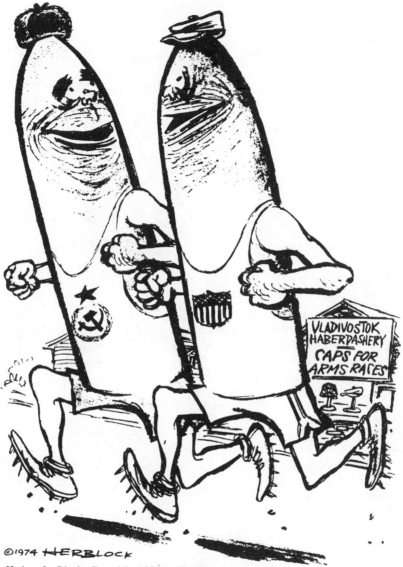

©1974 HERBLOCK

Herbert L. Block. Copyright 1974 by Herblock for The Washington Post.

"As Soon as Mirv is Ready, He'll Go to the Conference with You."

Herbert L. Block. Copyright 1969 by Herblock for The Washington Post.

Particularly worrying to some was the problem of multiple-warhead missiles (called MIRVs, for multiple independently targetable reentry vehicles). Despite fears that they would further destabilize the arms race, the Senate voted to begin testing MIRVs in 1969, just as the SALT talks were getting under way.

"I'm Not Sure of the Rules, but It Looks Like an Interesting Game."

Hugh Haynie. Copyright © Courier-Journal, Louisville Times Co. Reprinted with permission.

At the same time the administration was making peace overtures to Moscow, it began secretly courting Beijing. Nixon hoped Chinese pressure on North Vietnam could hasten the end of the war; he also anticipated trading advantages and balance-of-power dividends from consorting with the Soviet Union's archenemy.

The tricky part was maintaining traditionally good U.S. relations with Taiwan (and its conservative supporters at home) since both the People's Republic of China and Taiwan claimed to be the sole China.

"I Suppose You're Going to Tell Me You were out Building Bridges Again. . . ."

Don Wright. Reprinted by permission: Tribune Media Services.

China's Membership in the United Nations: A New Seating Plan?

Don Wright. Reprinted by permission: Tribune Media Services.

Over U.S. objections, the PRC was admitted to the UN in 1971. Nixon visited China in 1972, and by the time he left office, the stage was set for full normalization of U.S.–PRC relations, which occurred under President Jimmy Carter seven years later.

That Makes It Legitimate?

Karl Hubenthal. Los Angeles Herald Examiner.

Nixon's successor, Gerald Ford, tried to build on the arms control achievements of SALT I, but his efforts met with increasing resistance from conservatives. Many were incensed by the United States' participation in the Helsinki accords, signed by thirty-five nations in 1975, which in effect accepted the postwar boundaries in Eastern Europe in return for Moscow's promise to improve its human rights record. Under attack from his party's right wing, Ford banished the term *détente* from his vocabulary in his unsuccessful bid for reelection in 1976.

Jimmy Carter, however, had high hopes for détente when he took office in 1977. Dissatisfied with the limited achievements, as he viewed them, of SALT I, Carter set out to slash nuclear weapons arsenals in the SALT II talks. He

Ed Gamble. Reprinted with special permission of King Features Syndicate, Inc.

Bob Gorrell. Reprinted with special permission of North America Syndicate, Inc.

Bob Gorrell. Reprinted with special permission of North America Syndicate, Inc.

Don Wright. Reprinted by permission: Tribune Media Services.

Don Wright. Reprinted by permission: Tribune Media Services.

Mark Taylor. Albuquerque Tribune. Rothco.

generally downplayed East–West relations in order to concentrate more on "North–South" issues. He was scorned by conservative Republicans—but also met stiff resistance on SALT II from members of his own party, especially Senator Henry "Scoop" Jackson of Washington. Senate approval of SALT II, signed in 1977, was going to require compromises.

Carter's own attitude toward the Soviets and the wisdom of signing a treaty

Mike Peters. Copyright © 1980 Dayton Daily News. By permission of United Feature Syndicate, Inc.

with them changed dramatically by the end of his term in office, after the Soviets involved themselves in civil wars in Africa directly or through Cuban proxies. The 1979 "discovery" of a Soviet brigade in Cuba (which some pointed out had been there since at least 1976) and the Soviet invasion of Afghanistan later that year were the last straws, killing any chance for Senate approval of SALT II. Carter pulled the United States out of the 1980 Moscow Olympics and the allies

Jeff MacNelly. Reprinted by permission: Tribune Media Services.

Slow Learner

Jim Borgman. Reprinted with special permission of King Features Syndicate, Inc.

Chuck Ayers. Akron Beacon Journal. Reprinted by permission.

followed suit. He also canceled a signed agreement to sell grain to Moscow. In his last budget, he and his defense secretary, Harold Brown, raised defense spending considerably. But his move came too late to salvage the election; Carter had developed a reputation for weakness in the face of Soviet expansion, and he lost in a landslide to conservative Ronald Reagan in 1980.

9

The "Muddle" East

Carter had a good deal more on his plate than relations with the Soviet Union. One overriding priority was to seek a solution to the nearly thirty-year-old—and frequently lethal—enmity between Israel and its Arab neighbors.

Carter was hardly the first U.S. president to tackle the region's problems. Crucial because of its oil wealth, the Middle East had been a major arena in the superpower competition since World War II. By the mid-1960s it was a "powder keg," in Nixon's words, with the Arabs heavily armed by the Soviets and the Israelis by the French. It was also home to hundreds of thousands of Palestinian Arab refugees, many of whom banded together in 1964 to form the Palestine

WHICH CAME FIRST...

...THE CHICKEN OR THE EGG?

Ben Sargent. Austin American Statesman. Reprinted with permission. All rights reserved.

Bob Englehart. The Hartford Courant. Reprinted with permission.

Mike Keefe. The Denver Post. Reprinted with permission.

" 'Scuse Please—New Delivery!"

Pat Oliphant. Copyright © 1971 Universal Press Syndicate. All rights reserved.

Liberation Organization. The PLO dedicated itself, with the support of many Arab nations (most of whom, however, did not want the guerrillas on their soil), to the elimination of Israel and the creation of a Palestinian state. Although his political star has all but vanished periodically, Yasir Arafat still heads the PLO, as he has since 1968.

The Israelis trounced their neighbors in the 1967 Six-Day War, acquiring vast new real estate in the process: the entire Sinai Peninsula and the Gaza Strip from Egypt, the Golan Heights from Syria, and the West Bank of the Jordan River (including the Arab half of Jerusalem) from Jordan. Under the terms of UN Resolution 242, Israel offered to return the territories if their former owners would explicitly recognize Israel's right to exist within secure boundaries. The Arabs, however, refused to recognize, negotiate with, or make peace with Israel.

Over the next several years, while Soviet and U.S. military supplies poured into the region, there was intermittent fighting as Egypt attempted to regain the Sinai. Nixon's secretary of state, William P. Rogers, managed to arrange a cease-fire in 1970, but the administration's attempts to secure a more lasting peace proved futile.

"Jump off and You'll Get a Lifetime Supply of Shark Repellent."

Bill Mauldin. Reprinted with special permission of North America Syndicate, Inc.

Tony Auth. Philadelphia Inquirer. Copyright © 1972. Reprinted with permission of Universal Press Syndicate. All rights reserved.

"There Goes the 8:05"

Don Wright. Reprinted by permission: Tribune Media Services.

"Blessed is the Peacemaker . . . for He Shall Make Billions."

Paul Szep. Reprinted courtesy of The Boston Globe.

In 1972, President Anwar al-Sadat startled Moscow and Washington by informing his Soviet guests, who had refused his request for additional arms, that they were no longer welcome. Egypt was preparing for a major new assault on Israel, which it launched with Syria in October 1973. Caught by surprise, Israel initially lost territory until the United States stepped up its aid. This time it took two years of shuttle diplomacy by national security adviser Kissinger and promises of huge increases in U.S. military and economic aid to both Israel and

"Frankly, I Didn't Think We were That Close to an Agreement"

Don Wright. Reprinted by permission: Tribune Media Services.

Egypt to produce a cease-fire. A stable peace, however, still eluded the negotiators.

Carter, from the start of his administration, committed his energies and political reputation to the peace process. Sadat provided an opening with his

Pat Oliphant. Copyright © 1978 Universal Press Syndicate. Reprinted with permission. All rights reserved.

historic visit to Israeli prime minister Menachem Begin in 1977. Carter hosted Sadat and Begin at Camp David in 1978, where they hammered out the terms of a peace treaty—the first and only one to date between Israel and an Arab nation—that was finally signed in March 1979. Under its terms, Israel returned

Old Friends of the Groom

Draper Hill. Copyright © 1978, Draper Hill, in The Detroit News.

the Sinai to Egypt in 1982 and promised to grant limited autonomy to Palestinians living in the occupied territories over a period of five years. For his part in the peace, which made no provision for a Palestinian homeland, Sadat was ostracized by Egypt's former allies. He was assassinated two years later.

The part of the treaty calling for Palestinian autonomy was not realized within anything like five years. Instead, Israelis began establishing new settlements on the occupied West Bank, with the help of subsidies from the Begin government.

"Don't Anybody Panic! We Lost Our Pilot, but Mr. Mubarak Here Thinks He Can Fly the Plane!"

Ed Gamble. Reprinted with special permission of King Features Syndicate, Inc.

"What D'Ya Mean I Don't Know How the Game is Played?"

Mark Taylor. Albuquerque Tribune. Rothco.

Paul Conrad. Copyright © 1981 Los Angeles Times Syndicate. Reprinted by permission.

Begin and many others believed that because the West Bank ("Judea and Samaria") was part of the biblical Land of Israel, it should never be returned to the Arabs. Begin's Likud party also continued to insist that a return to Israel's pre-1967 borders would leave Israel defenseless against the Arabs.

Jim Morin. Reprinted with special permission of King Features Syndicate, Inc.

From bases in southern Lebanon the PLO, with Syrian support, launched repeated attacks against northern Israel. In keeping with its policy of holding host countries responsible for such attacks, Israel invaded southern Lebanon in 1978, withdrawing three months later. But PLO attacks continued, and in 1982

Don Wright. Reprinted by permission: Tribune Media Services.

Tony Auth. Philadelphia Inquirer. Copyright © 1989. Reprinted with permission of Universal Press Syndicate. All rights reserved.

Mike Keefe. The Denver Post. Reprinted with permission.

Israeli troops invaded Lebanon and drove all the way to Beirut in an attempt to root out the PLO for good. Ronald Reagan sent U.S. marines to Beirut to join a multilateral peacekeeping force that was to oversee Arafat's evacuation and then to help the Lebanese government reassert authority over its war-torn territory. But it was an impossible job in a country where seemingly everyone was at war with everyone else: Lebanese Christians against Lebanese Muslims, Syrians against Israelis, moderates against extremists. The presence of the marines, caught in the cross fire, grew increasingly unpopular at home. In October 1983, 241 marines were killed in their beds by a suicide truck bomb mission. Reagan brought the troops home in early 1984.

Lee Judge. Kansas City Times. Reprinted with permission.

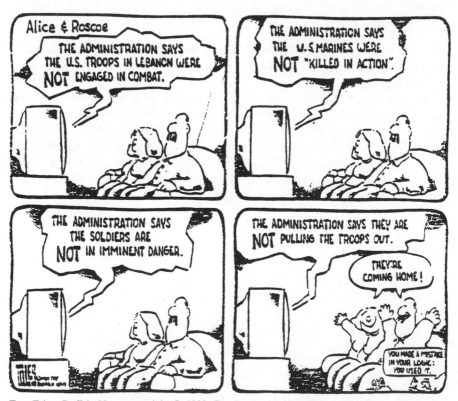

Tom Toles, Buffalo News copyright © 1989. Reprinted with permission. All rights reserved.

The Phoenix

Jim Borgman. Reprinted with special permission of King Features Syndicate, Inc.

Though Arafat was expelled from Lebanon in 1982, he set up new quarters in Tunisia, where he helped coordinate the December 1987 uprising or *intifadah* on the West Bank against the Israeli authorities. As the death toll from the intifadah rose, Israeli liberals and many Americans looked to Washington to take a more active role in seeking peace. As a first step they urged the U.S. government to drop its ban on negotiating with the PLO. At the very end of the Reagan administration, the PLO grudgingly declared that it accepted Israel's right to exist and that it would renounce terrorism; the United States announced that it

Mike Luckovich. By permission of Mike Luckovich and Creators Syndicate.

Steve Greenberg. Seattle Post-Intelligencer.

Mike Keefe. The Denver Post. Reprinted with permission.

"And the Usual Gunfire and Tear Gas around Bethlehem . . ."

Paul Rigby, New York Daily News. Reprinted with permission of Copley News Service.

would begin talks with PLO representatives. The Israeli government, however, continued to refuse to deal with the PLO, convinced that it had not changed its stripes. Christmas 1988 in the Holy Land did not look much different from any other Christmas in recent times.

10

The Unruly Third World

Vietnam and the Middle East were not the only hard lessons the United States learned in the 1970s about the limits of its ability to order the world as it might have liked. The Third World of developing nations was increasingly a place of

Tony Auth. Philadelphia Inquirer.
Copyright © 1978. Reprinted with
permission of Universal Press Syndicate. All rights reserved.

Wizard of Id

Brant Parker. Reprinted with special permission of King Features Syndicate, Inc.

Don Wright. Reprinted by permission: Tribune Media Services.

instability and unpredictability, and the United States soon discovered just how exposed it was to developments far from home.

The oil crisis of 1973 was a rude shock. The Arab nations and other major oil producers had banded together in the Organization of Petroleum Exporting Countries. In 1973, OPEC's Arab members embargoed oil sales to the United States in retaliation for American support for Israel in the October war and quadrupled the price of oil on the world market.

In the UN, where the Third World by now greatly outnumbered the industrialized West and its allies, anti-Americanism was on the rise and so was anti-Israeli sentiment, which the OPEC nations fanned into flames in the General Assembly.

Jeff MacNelly. Reprinted by permission: Tribune Media Services.

Draper Hill. Copyright © 1974, Draper Hill, in The Commercial
Appeal (Memphis).

Mike Peters. Copyright © 1977 Dayton Daily News. By permission of United Feature
Syndicate, Inc.

Tony Auth. Philadelphia Inquirer. Copyright © 1978. Reprinted with permission of Universal Press
Syndicate. All rights reserved.

Of Course, I'd Resign at Once if I Thought
for a Moment They Really Meant It!

Pat Oliphant. Copyright © 1979 Universal Press Syndicate. Reprinted with permission.
All rights reserved.

By 1976 America's self-confidence was low, wounded by Vietnam, Watergate, the oil crisis and a concurrent recession. Jimmy Carter, former governor of Georgia, won the 1976 presidential election in part because he was a Washington outsider who appealed to the voters with his calls for an open, noninterventionist foreign policy, a downplaying of the U.S.–Soviet confrontation, and an emphasis on human rights.

In practice, however, Carter found himself constrained to continue many of the policies he had inherited and to be selective in imposing his standards on others. He maintained the friendship, forged by earlier administrations, with oil-rich Iran, whose jails were kept full by the shah's notorious secret police. In Latin America, where nations were far less willing than in the past to follow the U.S. lead in foreign policy, Carter provided aid to some governments known for human rights abuses while withdrawing it from others.

"My People Have Supported Me for over Forty Years."

Dennis Renault. Sacramento Bee. Rothco.

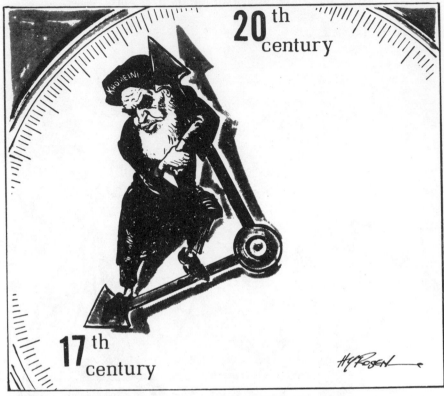

Hy Rosen. Copyright © 1979 by Hy Rosen, The Times-Union (Albany, N.Y.).

Despite a strong U.S. campaign to defeat it, in 1975 the assembly passed a resolution condemning Zionism as a form of racism. In the United States, support for the New York City-based institution plummeted.

A consistent foreign policy was also hard to chart, given the feuding between Carter's top two foreign policy advisers, Secretary of State Cyrus Vance (supported by U.S. Representative to the UN Andrew Young) and national security adviser Zbigniew Brzezinski.

Carter confronted a rising tide of revolution in the Third World. In Nicaragua, the dictator Anastasio Somoza Debayle, who had enjoyed the support of the United States for years, was overthrown, and soon thereafter the Sandinista revolution made a sharp turn to the left. In Iran, the shah was overthrown and before long Iraq attacked its presumably weakened neighbor. The war continued for eight years (1980–88); both sides suffered heavy casualties. The shah was succeeded by the rabidly anti-American Ayatollah Ruhollah Khomeini, whose goal was to extend his harsh, fundamentalist Islamic revolution throughout the Middle East. Terrorism became the new way to conduct business.

When Carter buckled to pressure from Kissinger and others to let the dying shah come to New York for medical treatment, he set the stage for his own undoing. Iranian students seized the U.S. embassy in Tehran; they held fifty-two Americans hostage for 444 days. The hostages were released on the day of Ronald Reagan's inauguration in January 1981.

Mike Peters. Copyright © 1979 Dayton Daily News. By permission of United Feature Syndicate, Inc.

Jim Morin. Reprinted with special permission of King Features Syndicate, Inc.

Jack Ohman. Reprinted by permission: Tribune Media Services.

11

Ronald Reagan and the "Evil Empire"

The fortieth president of the United States took office determined to restore American stature, which had suffered as a result of Communist inroads in Central America, the Iran hostage crisis, and the Soviet invasion of Afghanistan in December 1979. Ronald Wilson Reagan came out swinging, calling the Soviet Union an "evil empire" whose leaders were willing "to commit any crime, to lie, to cheat" in order to advance the cause of communism.

To counter the Soviet threat and the image of U.S. paralysis, Reagan set out to rebuild the military, which he pronounced "absolutely incapable of defending this country" as a result of the "neglect" of the Carter years. Only from a position of strength, Reagan believed, could the United States discourage the Soviets from Third World adventurism and convince them to make concessions

Jeff MacNelly. Reprinted by permission: Tribune Media Services.

"I Didn't Realize He'd Have Such a Comprehensive Approach to Foreign Affairs."

Herbert L. Block. Copyright 1984 by Herblock for The Washington Post.

Bill DeOre. Dallas Morning News. Reprinted by permission.

Mike Keefe. The Denver Post. Reprinted with permission.

Eldon Pletcher. Times-Picayune. Rothco.

Steve Kelley. San Diego Union. Reprinted with permission of Copley News Service.

It's Not Easy

Jack Ohman. Reprinted by permission: Tribune Media Services.

in nuclear arms control negotiations. It took a while, however, for his cabinet to get its foreign policy signals straight; frequent turnover in the leading foreign policy jobs did not help.

In his first five years in office, Reagan spent more than a trillion dollars on defense, hoping to equip the U.S. armed forces to meet Soviet aggression anywhere—a proposition critics found unrealistic; they said it would weaken the economy and thus hurt U.S. national security. The army, navy, and air force all received funds for advanced and expensive new weapons systems, not all of which worked quite as advertised.

Mike Keefe. The Denver Post. Reprinted with permission.

In the continuing struggle to make the United States' nuclear deterrent stronger, Reagan won funding to build a new intercontinental ballistic missile, the MX. But his administration, like its predecessor, was unable to come up with a survivable basing mode that satisfied Congress.

Reagan also launched the Strategic Defense Initiative, promptly dubbed Star Wars by the press. Reagan's aim was to build a shield that would make the enemy's nuclear weapons "impotent and obsolete"; his critics believed the plan was a technological mirage, would cost far too much, and would torpedo chances for arms control.

Tony Auth. Philadelphia Inquirer. Copyright © 1982. Reprinted with permission of Universal Press Syndicate. All rights reserved.

Steve Greenberg, Seattle Post-Intelligencer.

Jeff Danziger in The Christian Science Monitor copyright © 1984 TCSPS.

As the weapons buildup progressed, a string of horror stories about waste, fraud, and mismanagement among the Pentagon's chief defense contractors appeared in the press. Among the more outrageous examples of waste were a $7600 coffeepot and a $640 toilet seat.

"That's Our Boy"

Herbert L. Block. Copyright 1985 by Herblock for The Washington Post.

Wayne Stayskal. Reprinted by permission: Tribune Media Services.

While the buildup continued, arms control talks ground to a halt. In the absence of an agreement, the United States was prepared to deploy new intermediate-range nuclear forces (INF) in Western Europe in 1983 to counter those the Soviet Union had aimed in Europe's direction since the late 1970s. As the deployment deadline grew closer, antinuclear demonstrators took to the streets in European and U.S. cities, creating tensions within NATO. At that point the United States launched its 1982 "zero option" proposal, offering to cancel the deployment of new U.S. INF weapons if the Soviets would dismantle all of theirs. Few expected Moscow to agree; the idea was to quiet the burgeoning peace movement.

Gary Brookins. Richmond Times-Dispatch.

"Oh, Sure, You'll Always Have Your Fringe Element..."

Jim Borgman. Reprinted with special permission of King Features Syndicate, Inc.

John Trever. Albuquerque Journal. Reprinted with permission.

"I've Had Him on my Back Enough . . . Now You Take Him!"

Ed Gamble. Reprinted with special permission of King Features Syndicate, Inc.

Steve Kelley. San Diego Union. Reprinted with permission of Copley News Service.

Reagan was having other troubles with his NATO allies, who took exception to his rigidly hostile approach to the Soviet Union. Tempers flared in 1982 over a deal under which West European nations were to help Moscow build a natural gas pipeline that would benefit them considerably once it was built. The administration tried to talk its allies out of the deal, and, when that failed, imposed economic sanctions. The dispute was particularly divisive because the United States at the time was selling large quantities of grain to Moscow. Washington eventually backed down.

Don Wright. Reprinted by permission: Tribune Media Services.

Feiffer

Copyright © 1982 Jules Feiffer. Reprinted with permission Universal Press Syndicate. All rights reserved.

One of the obstacles to arms control lay in the Kremlin, where Brezhnev's death in 1982 led to a succession crisis. Brezhnev was followed in the top Communist party job by Yuri Andropov, sixty-eight, whose own ill health claimed him fifteen months later. Next came Constantin Chernenko, who lasted only thirteen months. Until Mikhail Gorbachev's accession in 1985, the top leadership in the USSR seemed paralyzed, locked into whatever policies had previously been set.

Jeff MacNelly. Reprinted by permission: Tribune Media Services.

Reprinted by permission: Tribune Media Services.

Yardwork in Central America

A major Reagan preoccupation throughout his eight years in office was the threat of Communist insurgencies in the U.S. "backyard" of Central America. Tiny, poor El Salvador was selected as the first test case for the fight, and early in its

Tony Auth. Philadelphia Inquirer. Copyright © 1983. Reprinted with permission of Universal Press

Doonesbury

Garry Trudeau. Copyright © 1981 G.B. Trudeau. Reprinted with permission of Universal Press Syndicate. All rights reserved.

Ben Sargent. Austin American Statesman. Reprinted with permission. All rights reserved.

first term, the administration issued a white paper documenting Soviet, Cuban, and Nicaraguan support for left-wing rebels there. El Salvador, which was run by a rightist dictatorship that kept order largely through the use of death squads, did not seem to administration critics the sort of government the United States ought to be supporting. Under pressure from Congress, the Reagan administration agreed to withhold aid if the government in San Salvador did not improve its human rights record. Although the United States spent hundreds of millions of dollars to help elect and support a moderate president, José Napoleón Duarte, by the end of 1988 a new government associated with the right-wing death squads appeared on the verge of taking over.

DIPLOMACY

Sack. Reprinted by permission: Tribune Media Services.

Reagan's principal anti-Communist focus in Central America for most of his years in office, however, was not El Salvador but Nicaragua, where he supplied counterrevolutionaries (known as contras) with as much military and economic assistance as Congress would authorize—and then some. Critics charged that in his preoccupation with the Communist threat he was overlooking the real causes of revolution, which were economic and social, and that he was too partial to military solutions at the expense of diplomatic options. Congress, it seemed, could not make up its mind whether it wanted to fund the contras or not: sometimes it gave military aid, sometimes only humanitarian, and sometimes none at all. Congressional indecision was due in part to the serious reservations

David Horsey, Seattle Post-Intelligencer.

Steve Greenberg, Seattle Post-Intelligencer.

Meddick. Copyright © 1986 Newspaper Enterprise Association, Inc.

Steve Turtil. Rothco.

Ed Gamble. Reprinted with special permission of King Features Syndicate, Inc.

Mike Keefe. The Denver Post. Reprinted with permission.

many legislators had about the contras. While Reagan equated them with the U.S. Founding Fathers, critics saw them in a far less favorable light. Many also doubted they could win. Nicaraguan President Daniel Ortega Saavedra's behavior unintentionally helped the contras' case: a scant week after Congress

Nicaragua Admitted Today to the Mining of New York Harbor to Force the U.S. to Change its Government to One More Acceptable to Managua.

Doug Marlette. Reprinted with special permission of King Features Syndicate, Inc.

Tony Auth. Philadelphia Inquirer. Copyright © 1986. Reprinted with permission of Universal Press Syndicate. All rights reserved.

Powell. Copyright © 1983 Los Angeles Times Syndicate. Reprinted by permission.

voted to withhold contra funding in 1986, Ortega paid a visit to Moscow to request more aid.

The administration, warning that the fate of democracy in the region was at stake, resorted to illegal aid and other activities to keep the contras afloat. When it mined Nicaragua's harbors in 1983, the administration provoked outrage at home and abroad. It then compounded the international community's contempt when it refused the jurisdiction of the World Court in the case.

In 1983, the United States invaded the small Caribbean island of Grenada to rescue American students there when a power struggle in the leftist government turned violent. The operation earned mixed reviews: the administration claimed (although Cuba denied it) that it had prevented the island from becoming a Soviet and Cuban military base. Others were less impressed.

The administration's continued attempts to overthrow the Sandinista government by arming the contras culminated in the worst scandal to hit the White House since Watergate. In 1986, the press revealed that administration officials had secretly sold arms to the Iranian government and illegally funneled some of the funds (those that were not skimmed by the brokers of the deal) to the contras. Officials who had participated in the scheme—among them national security advisers Robert C. MacFarlane and John Poindexter and their aide Col. Oliver North—said they were protecting vital U.S. interests in the face of unwarranted congressional meddling and indecision. Reagan's role in the scheme was never fully determined.

Gene Bassett. Copyright © 1983 United Feature Syndicate, Inc.

Signe Wilkinson. San Jose Mercury News. Reprinted by permission.

Steve Benson. Reprinted by permission: Tribune Media Services.

"What Do I Know . . . And When Will I Know It?"

Bill Shorr. Copyright © 1987 Los Angeles Times Syndicate. Reprinted by permission.

13

Gorby

Reagan recovered from the Iran-contra scandal with help from a surprising quarter—the new Soviet leader Mikhail Gorbachev, who took power in 1985 and put a new face on Soviet foreign policy. In 1986, Gorbachev and Reagan met in

David Locher. Reprinted by permission: Tribune Media Services.

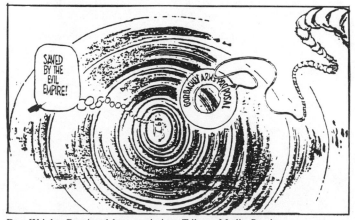

Don Wright. Reprinted by permission: Tribune Media Services.

Tom Toles, Buffalo News copyright 1989. Reprinted with permission. All rights reserved.

Reykjavik, Iceland, and, in a move that caught the West off guard, Gorbachev suggested radical cuts in nuclear arsenals. Subsequent negotiations led to the 1987 INF (intermediate-range nuclear forces) treaty, the first arms control agreement to eliminate an entire class of nuclear missiles. The Senate approved it—despite conservative opposition led by Jesse Helms (R–N.C.)—in 1988.

MISSILE
WITH
WARHEAD

NUKE
THE
INF
TREATY!

HELMS

Linda Boileau. Frankfort State Journal. Rothco.

Sure, We're a Police State...But Now We're a *Nice* Police State.

Henry Payne. Copyright 1987 Scripps Howard Newspapers.

The Dashing New Jockey, Gorbachev, and His Sleek Thoroughbred.

Henry Payne. Copyright © 1987 Scripps Howard Newspapers.

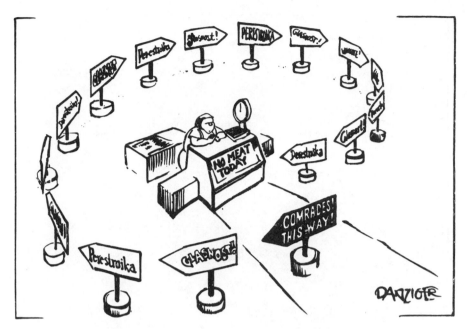

Jeff Danziger in The Christian Science Monitor copyright 1988 TCSPS.

At home, Gorbachev was enacting reforms that astounded observers in the United States. Under his new policy of *glasnost* (openness) he encouraged wider debate in the press, freed a number of dissidents from Soviet jails, and allowed others to emigrate. American conservatives were still not impressed. Gorbachev also initiated a radical restructuring *(perestroika)* he hoped would turn the stagnant Soviet economy around, but there were few immediate results apparent to average Soviet citizens. To save money and patch up quarrels with the West, Gorbachev announced that he would cut Soviet military spending. At the end of 1988 he offered to cut Soviet ground troops in Europe by 50 percent and retain only what he referred to as military "sufficiency" in Europe. Conservatives remained skeptical.

Gorbachev also pulled Soviet troops out of Afghanistan, after a disastrous nine-year war, and became notably less eager to bankroll clients in the Third World. Editorial writers speculated that the cold war era might be coming to a close.

Dan Wasserman. Copyright © 1988 Los Angeles Times Syndicate. Reprinted by permission.

Steve Benson. Reprinted by permission: Tribune Media Services.

But Aside from That, Sir, How Do You Like Afghanistan?

Jeff Danziger in The Christian Science Monitor copyright © 1988 TCSPS.

Gorbachev consolidated his control over the government during his first few years in office, but not without challenges: glasnost and perestroika were encouraging the expression of all kinds of grievances, including demands for more autonomy from republics around the edges of the Soviet Union. Observers in the United States wondered whether the winds of change Gorbachev had unleashed would blow him away.

Ed Gamble. Reprinted with special permission of King Features Syndicate, Inc.

Democracy Comes to the Soviet Union.

Jeff MacNelly. Reprinted by permission: Tribune Media Services.

Henry Payne. Copyright © 1988 Scripps Howard Newspapers.

Scott Stantis. Reprinted by permission of The Commercial Appeal (Memphis).

14
Terrorism: Scourge of the Eighties

When Ronald Reagan welcomed the hostages home from Iran shortly after his inauguration, he warned: "Let terrorists be aware that when the rules of international behavior are violated, our policy will be one of swift and effective retribution." His administration announced that it would not make concessions

Ed Gamble. Reprinted with special permission of King Features Syndicate, Inc.

Steve Barling in The Christian Science Monitor copyright © 1985 TCSPS.

to, pay ransom to, or negotiate with terrorists for the release of hostages and said that when possible it would consider "means of active prevention, preemption and retaliation." That, of course, required identifying and locating those responsible.

It soon became apparent, however, that the United States was unable to back up its rhetoric. Beirut, Lebanon, became Terrorism Central: the bombing of the U.S. embassy there was followed by the truck bombing of the marine barracks that killed 241; and Americans (as well as citizens of other countries) living in

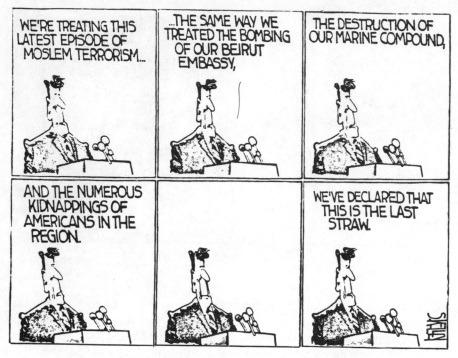

Steve Kelley. San Diego Union. Reprinted by permission of Copley News Service.

Mike Peters. Copyright © 1988 Dayton Daily News. By permission of United Feature Syndicate, Inc.

Beirut were kidnapped off the streets, probably by Shiite terrorists believed to be affiliated with Khomeini's Iran. The hostages still in captivity at the end of the Reagan administration included Terry Waite, a British minister who had visited

Beirut several times in an attempt to negotiate their release before he became a hostage himself.

The year 1985 was especially grim. Within one month a major airport in West

David Horsey. Seattle Post-Intelligencer.

Don Wright. Reprinted by permission: Tribune Media Services.

Germany was bombed, an Air India jet with 329 people aboard was blown out of the sky by a Sikh's bomb, and a truckload of leftist guerrillas opened fire on a string of street cafés in El Salvador, killing a number of U.S. marines. Then the

Mark Alan Stamaty. Copyright © 1985 Mark Alan Stamaty. Reprinted from *The Village Voice* with permission of the artist.

world watched the two-week ordeal of those aboard TWA flight 847, hijacked by Shiite terrorists who had eluded security at the Athens airport. Before all those on board were freed, a U.S. navy diver had been murdered. Four months later, Palestinian terrorists hijacked a cruise ship, the *Achille Lauro,* and dumped an elderly infirm passenger overboard.

"Probably a Couple of Croissants and Some Rolls"

Herbert L. Block. Copyright © 1985 by Herblock for The Washington Post.

Ed Gamble. Reprinted with special permission of King Features Syndicate, Inc.

Tom Toles, Buffalo News copyright © 1989. Reprinted with permission. All rights reserved.

That year the United States began to list and censure countries known to sponsor terrorism. But administration critics pointed out that the list was selective: omitted were countries known to sponsor terrorism whose cooperation the United States needed—for example Syria, a major player in the Middle East. Critics also accused the administration of using terrorist tactics itself when they suited its purposes.

The United States was not without success in fighting terrorism, despite numerous frustrating failures. The U.S. bombing of Tripoli in 1986, for exam-

Bob Taylor. Reprinted with permission of the Dallas Times Herald.

Mike Keefe. The Denver Post. Reprinted with permission.

ple, was followed by a marked falloff in Libyan terrorist attacks. (The victims of the bombing raid, however, included a number of civilians, among them one of Libyan leader Muammar Qaddafi's children.) The United States also successfully captured the hijackers of the *Achille Lauro* in the summer of 1986.

Jim Morin. Reprinted with special permission of King Features Syndicate, Inc.

Steve Greenberg. Seattle Post-Intelligencer.

"So Far, So Good . . . What's Your Next Move Going to Be?"

Etta Hulme. Copyright © 1987 Fort Worth Star-Telegram. By permission of Newspaper Enterprise Association, Inc.

When the Iran-contra story broke, it became apparent that the administration had, behind the scenes, violated most of its ground rules for dealing with terrorism. Instead of refusing to negotiate with terrorists, Washington had secretly tried to strike a deal selling Iran arms and spare parts in exchange for the release of Americans held in Lebanon by Iranian allies.

15

Trade, the Deficit, and the Debt

In 1982 the United States, leader of the postwar economic world, became a debtor nation. By 1986 it had become the world's number-one debtor, and the federal budget deficit was continuing to grow, hitting the trillion-dollar mark at the end of 1988.

"I Don't Know Why They Don't Seem to Hold Us in Awe the Way They Used To."

Herbert L. Block. Copyright © 1987 by Herblock for The Washington Post.

"Take It Off! Take It All Off!!"

Pat Oliphant. Copyright 1971 Universal Press Syndicate. Reprinted with permission. All rights reserved.

"When the United States sneezes, Europe catches a cold," goes one saying. U.S. economic policies have long been a source of friction between America and its allies. One of the biggest shocks came in 1971 when, without warning, President Nixon devalued the dollar and ended the gold-exchange standard that had assured the stability of the international monetary system since World War II. The United States also imposed a surcharge on imports, over critics' protests that we were risking a trade war with our allies. But the administration charged that we had helped those allies back to their feet after the war only to have them try to price us out of the market by way of gratitude.

"And to Think I Set Him up in Business!"

Gib Crockett. Washington Star.

"You Hate Me When I'm Strong and Despise Me When I'm Weak."

Bill Mauldin. Reprinted with special permission of North America Syndicate, Inc.

The fluctuation in the dollar's value irritated U.S. allies and trading partners. Initially, however, it did little harm to the United States: the value of the dollar declined, making U.S. goods cheaper and more competitive abroad. But the

The Evolution Of American Labor

Bill DeOre. Dallas Morning News. Reprinted by permission.

Don Wright. Reprinted with permission: Tribune Media Services.

Jim Borgman. Reprinted with special permission of King Features Syndicate, Inc.

subsequent rise in the dollar's value made some U.S. goods too expensive to compete with exports. As factories here closed down, the affected industries and organized labor lobbied Washington for a new round of protectionist legislation. Much of American ire was directed against Japan, which sells much more to the United States than it buys. At the least, the protectionists argued, we should be allowed the same access to the Japanese market as the Japanese have here. Free traders, however, warned that protectionism would hurt more than help and urged the United States to get its economy in order and U.S. industry to make itself more competitive.

Draper Hill. Copyright © 1985, Draper Hill, in The Detroit News.

John Trever. Albuquerque Journal. Reprinted with permission.

"The Auto Import Quotas Gave Me Time to Get Ready to Compete Against You Again..."

Bruce Beattie. Reprinted by permission of Copley News Service.

"Hi! My name is Dr. Phinius T. Congress, and I'm Here to Help!"

Henry Payne. Copyright © 1987 Scripps Howard Newspapers.

Jeff MacNelly. Reprinted by permission: Tribune Media Services.

Sack. Reprinted by permission: Tribune Media Services.

Dan Wasserman. Copyright © 1985 Los Angeles Times Syndicate. Reprinted by permission.

Tom Toles, Buffalo News copyright © 1986. Reprinted with permission. All rights reserved.

Awash in red ink from the budget deficit and worsening balance of trade, the country had an attack of nerves. As investors scrambled to unload their stocks, the New York stock market average fell 508 points on Black Monday, October 19, 1987. The gloom was quickly reflected in falling markets around the globe.

The United States attempted to deal with its rising deficits through the Gramm–Rudman–Hollings Act, legislation that mandated budget cuts to reduce the deficit to zero over a period of years. But the measure seemed to lack teeth. It was politically easier for Washington to do nothing than to cut funding for popular programs.

Much of the deficit in recent years has been financed through the sale of U.S. securities to foreigners, both governments and wealthy individuals, attracted by relative U.S. economic stability and high interest rates. Foreign investors have also bought land and factories, looking for a larger share of the lucrative U.S. market.

In the meantime, a number of developing countries, particularly in Latin

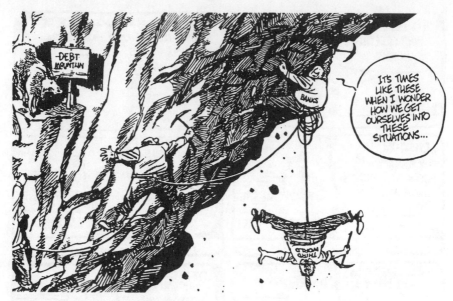

Henry Payne. Copyright © 1988 Scripps Howard Newspapers.

Dan Wasserman. Copyright © 1987 Los Angeles Times Syndicate. Reprinted by permission.

Open Season

Burges Green. The Providence Journal, 1966.

America, that borrowed heavily from U.S. banks during the 1960s and 1970s found themselves unable to keep up with the interest payments on their debt. When Mexico announced in 1982 that it was about to default, it sparked a debt crisis that persists to this day. Not only have U.S. banks lost money but, as Latin American buying power has weakened, the United States has also lost markets. The deficit has also affected U.S. development assistance: U.S. aid to the poorest countries, never a popular way to spend taxpayer dollars, has fallen. Even those who support aid in principle worry that it frequently winds up in the wrong hands.

Growing numbers of analysts were warning by the late 1980s that the age of U.S. economic preeminence was ending. They urged Washington to redefine its concept of national security, arguing that Washington's traditional emphasis on military defense had become anachronistic. What was needed now was an emphasis on educating the next generation to compete internationally. Otherwise, warned doomsayers, the next era will be Japan's.

"Now that Dollars are Worth Less, We'll Need More of Them."

Bill Mauldin. Reprinted with permission of North America Syndicate, Inc.

Mort Walker. Reprinted with special permission of King Features Syndicate, Inc.

Hirohito's Revenge

Paul Conrad. Copyright © 1985 Los Angeles Times Syndicate. Reprinted by permission.

16

Interdependence:
Love It or Go It Alone

The worldwide panic triggered by the stock market crash in October 1987 was graphic proof of the interconnectedness of economies around the world. Other problems that could only be solved if attacked globally were multiplying rapidly. A large hole in the ozone layer of the atmosphere, discovered over Antarctica, was raising the specter of higher levels of ultraviolet radiation and skin cancer on earth. The burning of fossil fuels and the felling of trees in dwindling tropical rain forests were producing a "greenhouse effect," making global warming a dangerous reality. Acid rain from industrial smokestacks was crossing national borders, ruining forests and lakes and the wildlife that depend on them.

The international drug traffic and the toll it was taking on American society constituted another problem that only grew worse with time. Despite his "Just Say No" campaign, however, Reagan was unable to claim any victories. International drug dealers continued to intimidate governments into at least tacit cooperation as in Colombia or, in the case of Gen. Manuel Noriega's Panama, ran the country themselves.

In the beginning, God created Heaven and earth ....

... and He created the seas ....

... and then, God made Man ....

There goes the neighborhood.

Jim Morin. Reprinted with special permission of King Features Syndicate, Inc.

Tom Meyer. Copyright © 1988 San Francisco Chronicle.
By permission of United Feature Syndicate, Inc.

ON THE SUNNY SIDE OF
OZONE LAYER DEPLETION

REVOLUTIONIZE OUTDOOR BARBECUES

CUT DOWN EXPENSIVE HEATING BILLS

TAN IN JUST MINUTES

Ben Wicks. Newhall Signal. Rothco.

Mike Peters. Copyright © 1988 Dayton Daily News. By permission of United Feature Syndicate, Inc.

Ben Wicks. Newhall Signal. Rothco.

"Maybe It Loses Something In Translation"

Etta Hulme. Copyright © 1988 Forth Worth Star-Telegram. By permission of Newspaper Enterprise Association, Inc.

Jim Morin. Reprinted with special permission of King Features Syndicate, Inc.

Jim Morin. Reprinted with special permission of King Features Syndicate, Inc.

Don Wright. Reprinted by permission: Tribune Media Services.

Steve Kelley. Reprinted by permission of Copley News Service.

Fallout from revolutions around the world was also leaving its mark at home as waves of immigrants, fleeing war or its aftermath in Latin America and Southeast Asia, tried to start a new life in the land of promise. The United States, a nation of immigrants, was forced to clamp down on the number of people it would accept.

The older unresolved problems remained. Despite the 1968 nuclear nonproliferation treaty, a growing number of countries who had refused to sign were getting their hands on the technology needed to build nuclear weapons. Wars were still disrupting the lives of millions, especially in the poorest countries. And rapid population growth meant more people were vying for scarce food in the most destitute parts of the world.

Given the growing need for international cooperation to tackle the problems on the global agenda, some thought there might be a greater role for the UN in years ahead—especially since the Soviet Union under Gorbachev appeared interested, for the first time in decades, in using the organization to solve international disputes. Others were skeptical.

Herbert L. Block. Copyright © 1987 by Herblock for The Washington Post.

Jimmy Margulies. Houston Post. Rothco.

"Guess What the Year 2074 will be Like?"

Al Liederman. Long Island Press (N.Y.). Rothco.

The Small Society

Morrie Brickman. Reprinted with special permission of King Features Syndicate, Inc.

"Please Pass the Ice Cream . . ."

Rob Rogers. Copyright 1985 The Pittsburgh Press. By permission of United Feature Syndicate, Inc.

By the end of 1988 the United States was facing a new administration, a new decade, and a new century. Much had changed since the last years of the nineteenth century: humankind had survived two world wars only to develop nuclear weapons that, if they failed to deter a third one, could wipe out the race that invented them within a matter of minutes. Economic advances had created both new opportunities and environmental hazards. The United States, which had been powerful enough to do as it chose for most of the 1900s, had found its freedom of action constrained by other countries and other forces as the twentieth century drew to a close.

Pogo

Walt Kelly. Copyright 1970, OGPI. Reprinted by permission of The Los Angeles Times Syndicate.

17

The Wall Crumbles

Jeff MacNelly. Reprinted by permission: Tribune Media Services.

In January 1989, while George Herbert Walker Bush was being sworn in as president of the United States, the changes Mikhail Gorbachev had initiated in the USSR were sending shock waves throughout the Soviet bloc. Glasnost and perestroika had detonated a time bomb in international affairs.

Communist economies were in trouble, and East Europeans, heartened by Gorbachev's calls for reform, were growing restive. Economic crisis provoked a revolution first in Poland, where the government of Gen. Wojciech Jaruzelski was forced to turn to Solidarity, the independent trade union it had outlawed eight years earlier, to head off a threatened wave of strikes.

"He Says He Can Fix It, but He Wants Time-and-a-Half, Two Extra Coffee Breaks, and a Seat on the Board of Directors!"

Bob Gorrell. Reprinted with special permission of North America Syndicate, Inc.

Dan Wasserman. Copyright © 1989 Los Angeles Times Syndicate. Reprinted by permission.

In the ensuing negotiations that lasted from early February to early April, Solidarity, under the leadership of Lech Walesa, won back its legal status and a government promise to hold elections that June. When the voting was done, the union had won almost every available seat, although the Communists arranged matters so that Jaruzelski would continue as president.

The Soviet Union experienced its first secret-ballot, multicandidate elections that March. The results were a blow to the Communist party: even where party candidates ran unopposed, in more than twenty cases their constituents voted them out of office by scratching their names off the ballot. Elsewhere, upset wins gave seats in the new Congress of People's Deputies to outspoken government critics.

Jeff Danziger in The Christian Science Monitor copyright 1977 TCSPS.

'Hold an Election, He Says . . . Let Our Comrades Choose Their Leaders, He Says . . . What Could Happen? He Says . . .'

Mike Peters. Copyright © 1989 Dayton Daily News. By permission of United Feature Syndicate, Inc.

Tony Auth. Philadelphia Inquirer. Copyright © 1989. Reprinted with permission of Universal Press Syndicate. All rights reserved.

Political and economic liberalization was under way in China, too, and observers in the West watched with a mixture of hope and worry as the world's Communist giants struggled. In May 1989 students in Beijing took over Tiananmen Square, demanding more political rights, and the world held its breath. After a heady few weeks, Chinese senior leader Deng Xiaoping cracked down with troops and tanks, killing students and hunting down their leaders. It was a grim reminder of what powerful Communist leaders could do if they felt too threatened.

That summer, economic conditions in the USSR grew steadily worse despite Gorbachev's ambitious reform program. In July, fed up with the lack of

Mike Luckovich. By permission of Mike Luckovich and Creators Syndicate.

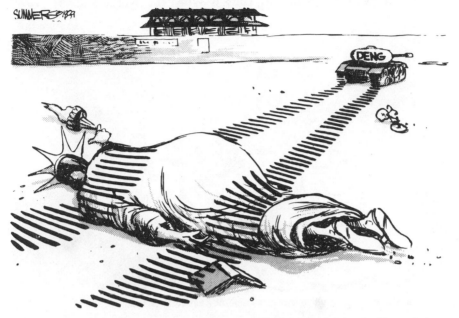

Dana Summers. Copyright © 1989, Washington Post Writers Group. Reprinted with permission.

decent food and even soap, almost 500,000 coal miners walked off the job. It cost the Kremlin nearly eight billion dollars (at the official exchange rate) in concessions to bring the striking miners back to work.

Meanwhile, ethnic unrest in the Soviet Union's many republics was getting worse. There was violence in Azerbaijan and Georgia. Moldavians and others demonstrated for the right to make their own languages official. The Baltic states

"Confidentially, Don't You Just Hate It When the Workers of the World Unite?"

Doug Marlette. Reprinted with special permission of King Features Syndicate, Inc.

Pat Oliphant. Copyright © 1989 Universal Press Syndicate. Reprinted with permission. All rights reserved.

Steve Kelley. Reprinted with permission of Copley News Service.

were demanding not only economic and cultural autonomy: Estonia, Latvia, and Lithuania were beginning to talk about outright independence from Moscow. Communist party hard-liners warned Gorbachev that he had sown the seeds of chaos.

Jeff Danziger in The Christian Science Monitor copyright 1989 TCSPS.

In Poland, General Jaruzelski and company were finding it difficult to put together a government and asked Walesa whether he would care to try. Walesa declined, preferring to remain the power behind the throne, but in August Solidarity's Tadeusz Mazowiecki became prime minister. The Polish Communist party had become the first to turn itself out of power.

In the United States, many wondered what George Bush was doing while all this was going on. An early review of East–West relations had led him to believe that no major change in policy was called for, but critics thought he was missing historic opportunities. Bush visited Eastern Europe over the summer and applauded

"It is Absolutely Essential That the U.S. Provide a Rock of Stability Round Which the Rest of the Alliance Can Rally"—U.S. Defense Secretary Dick Cheney in testimony to Congress.

Pat Oliphant. Copyright © 1989 Universal Press Syndicate. Reprinted with permission. All rights reserved.

A New Breeze Blowing

Jeff MacNelly. Reprinted with permission: Tribune Media Services.

Dan Foote. Copyright © 1989. Reprinted with permission of Dallas Times Herald.

Walt Handelsman. Reprinted with permission: Tribune Media Services.

the changes in Poland but offered only limited U.S. financial help. Not until October did the Bush administration take a new tack, declaring itself firmly on the side of reform in the Soviet bloc and ready to help.

As exciting as the first half of 1989 had been, the second half was about to blow holes through even the wildest predictions about what might happen in

"When Did They Put That There?"

Jim Borgman. Reprinted with special permission of King Features Syndicate, Inc.

Eastern Europe. Back in May, Hungary, which was moving toward a more democratic government with a free market economy, had begun dismantling its fortified border with Austria. That August, some 40,000 East Germans vacationing in Hungary chose not to return home, and the Hungarian government decided to let them head west. That started a flood: by early November some 167,000 East Germans—1 percent of the population—had left the country. Hoping to stop the hemorrhage of the nation's best and brightest, East Germany opened its borders on November 9, kicking off one of the century's great parties as East and West

Tom Meyer. Copyright © 1989 San Francisco Chronicle. By permission of United Features Syndicate, Inc.

Mike Peters. Copyright © 1989 Dayton Daily News. By permission of United Feature Syndicate, Inc.

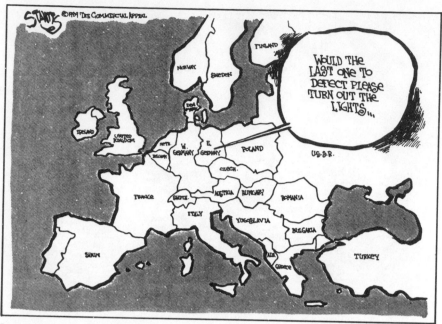

Scott Stantis. Reprinted by permission of The Commercial Appeal (Memphis).

Scrawls. Reprinted by permission of Newspaper Enterprise Association, Inc.

Rob Rogers. Copyright © 1989 The Pittsburgh Press. By permission of United Feature Syndicate, Inc.

Germans met atop the Berlin Wall. Some 40,000 East Germans visited West Berlin that weekend, mostly just to go shopping, and then returned home. But the East German Communist party was still in trouble, as weekly mass demonstrations made clear.

Dan Wasserman. Copyright © 1989 Los Angeles Times Syndicate. Reprinted by permission.

Hungary's Communist party had voted itself out of existence and renamed the country the Republic of Hungary in October. Poland had had a non-Communist leader since August. The Soviet Union remained calm.

And it still wasn't over. In November Bulgaria's hard-line strongman Todor Zhivkov was ousted and the Communist party in Czechoslovakia fell. By mid-December, East Germany, which had been one of the most repressive, antireform countries in Eastern Europe, had a non-Communist leader. Back in Washington, the President and his advisers decided a chat with Mr. Gorbachev was in order. What would the new Europe look like? Might Germany be reunited, and if so, would it be dangerous to the stability of Central Europe?

Someone's Been Sitting in My Chair, Eating My Porridge and Sleeping in My Bed, but Hey—I Can Live with That!"

Doug Marlette. Reprinted with special permission of King Features Syndicate, Inc.

Jim Borgman. Reprinted with special permission of King Features Syndicate, Inc.

Herbert L. Block. Copyright 1989 by Herblock for The Washington Post.

Tom Toles, Buffalo News copyright © 1989. Reprinted with permission. All rights reserved.

"What the Hell, Maybe It *Is* Time We Buried Lenin."

Jim Borgman. Reprinted with special permission of King Features Syndicate, Inc.

As the climate between the superpowers improved, U.S. businesses forged ahead with plans to take advantage of new markets in the East.

Bush and Gorbachev decided on a summit at sea in early December, off the coast of Malta. The press turned out in force, despite stormy weather, to report on the summit that could turn out to be the first of the post-Cold War era.

With the Cold War receding, the Pentagon began trying to figure out how to handle a drastically changed security situation in Europe.

Herbert L. Block. Copyright 1989 by Herblock for The Washington Post.

Bush is a Friendly but Go-slow Kind of Guy

Jim Morin. Reprinted with special permission of King Features Syndicate, Inc.

As statesmen contemplated the new era in U.S.-Soviet relations and politicians debated how to spend the "peace dividend," the first post-Cold War international crisis erupted. In the hot summer of 1990, Iraqi troops invaded Kuwait. The UN Security Council, including the United States, the Soviet Union, and the other permanent members, condemned Saddam Hussein's aggression. President Bush ordered U.S. troops to Saudi Arabia. It was the largest U.S. military buildup since the Vietnam War.

Dan Wasserman. Copyright © 1989 Los Angeles Times Syndicate. Reprinted by permission.

Ed Gamble. Reprinted with special permission of King Features Syndicate, Inc.

Tom Toles, Buffalo News copyright © 1989. Reprinted with permission. All rights reserved.

Walt Handelsman. Reprinted with permission: Tribune Media Services.

Mike Peters. Copyright © 1990 Dayton Daily News. By permission of United Feature Syndicate, Inc.

Index

Pharos Books are available at special discounts on bulk purchases for sales promotions, premiums, fundraising or educational use. For details, contact the Special Sales Department, Pharos Books, 200 Park Avenue, New York, NY 10166.